beauty /ˈbjudi/

noun

• that quality of a person or thing which is highly pleasing or satisfying to the mind; moral or intellectual excellence: *we ascribe beauty to that which is simple; which has no superfluous parts; which exactly answers its end.*

• that quality of a physical object or animal which is highly pleasing to the sight; perceived physical perfection; exceptional harmony of form or color: *a thing of beauty is a joy for ever: its loveliness increases; it will nevery pass into nothingness.*

• that quality of a thing which is highly pleasing to the senses generally: *the sombre beauty of evening, with its deep stillness broken only by the low moanings of affliction.*

verb

• to make beautiful or more beautiful; to adorn or decorate; to beautify: *zinnias and other colorful summer flowers beautied the rooms.*

Oxford English Dictionary, 3rd Edition

IN THIS ISSUE

LA+ BEAUTY
EDITORIAL

Upon opening this journal, you are greeted by a scene painted by Claude Monet, titled *Impression: Sunrise*. The hazy, atmospheric quality of the scene is characteristic of Monet's work, and that of other impressionist painters who worked with rapid brush strokes to capture the ephemeral qualities of light and color *en plein air*. The blurring of the painting's subject–the port of Monet's hometown of Le Havre–led him to give the painting the title *Impression*, as "it couldn't really be taken for a view of Le Havre."[1]

While the emergence of the Impressionist movement can be considered as reflective of a shift in stylistic preference in the late 19th century, a recent study suggests that something else was at play in its formation: the Industrial Revolution and associated proliferation of smog and air pollution in European cities. In that study, climate scientists Anna Lea Albright and Peter Huybers note the evident progression over time from object to blurred atmosphere in Monet's paintings. They also cite letters by the artist himself expressing his interest in and creative reliance on fog [the term 'smog' had not yet been created], "[W]hen I got up I was terrified to see that there was no fog, not even a wisp of mist: I was prostrate, and could just see all my paintings done for, but gradually the fires were lit and the smoke and haze came back."[2]

Viewing the endpapers of this issue may or may not feel different to you now, after becoming aware of this study. Does it matter if the impressionist haze of Monet's paintings was smog, or that he was relieved by the renewed presence of air pollution, which, centuries later, has amalgamated to create the climate crisis we now face? Is *Impression: Sunrise* less beautiful as a result?

There is of course no definitive or correct answer, and our respective answers likely differ. Beauty as a term and concept is complex and enigmatic, and it evades concrete definition. It can be appreciated visually and intellectually, taking on different forms and meanings in different cultures and contexts. It is the elusive nature of beauty's definition that serves as the point of departure for this issue of *LA+*.

This issue opens with a piece by Mariagrazia Portera, in which she explores the philosophical evolution of our understanding of beauty in the context of biological evolution and our present climate crisis. As humans, we are deeply entangled within our environment – perhaps more so than any other species, as our efforts to shape it to meet our needs and desires grip the entire planet. In return, this planetary crisis will inevitably shape us and pose not only existential but also aesthetic questions and dilemmas as environments change and species migrate and evolve to adapt to a warming world.

Perhaps, then, beauty in our present time isn't benevolent, peaceful, or comforting – the limited definition and framework simply does not accommodate the depth and breadth of unpredictable environmental change to come. Yet the notion of beauty as something other than peaceful or comforting also has its place in history and mythology, as Luke Morgan writes in his piece centered on the enchantress Circe.

Opposite: Photographer Dan Piech spent four years searching every section of sidewalk in Manhattan to document accidental moments of overlooked beauty going unnoticed beneath New Yorkers' feet.

1 Paul Smith, *Impressionism: Beneath the Surface* [H.N. Abrams, 1994].

2 Elaine Velie, "Did Air Pollution Inspire Impressionism?" Hyperallergic [February 7, 2023], https://hyperallergic.com/796492/did-air-pollution-inspire-impressionism/; "'I Find London Lovelier to Paint Each Day' – Claude Monet in London," Tate [September 12, 2017], https://www.tate.org.uk/tate-etc/issue-41-autumn-2017/claude-monet-i-find-london-lovelier-paint-each-day.

In it, landscape beauty carries a negative connotation – one of a false paradise, false nature, and entrapment. Beauty becomes suspect: what is beautiful is also potentially dangerous.

The range of what may be considered a beautiful landscape is explored by Gretchen Henderson through her discussion of Utah's Great Salt Lake and its tar seeps, a complex and harsh ecosystem surrounded by strip mines, military testing sites, and suburban sprawl. Henderson's research into the aesthetics of place is specifically situated in between the binaries of beauty and ugliness so as to broaden our perception of what can constitute environmental beauty. In her work, as with many of the authors in this issue, we can start to see the emergence of a new kind of landscape beauty, one that picks up where Robert Smithson left off.

Nevertheless, old images of landscape beauty are powerfully lodged in the public imagination. But as Dan van der Horst and Saskia Vermeylen write in their study of scenic value and windfarms, the notion of what constitutes an "eyesore" varies greatly depending upon one's frame of reference. In this regard, Sarem Sunderland writes of a massive early-20th-century Swiss hydroelectric landscape designed in its entirety to conform to an artist's landscape drawing of a beautiful alpine lake.

Beyond exploring questions of what can be considered beautiful, this issue also questions whose interests ideals of beauty serve. In their examination of the 606 and the proposed El Paseo trail in Chicago, Winifred Curran, Michelle Stuhlmacher, and Elsa Anderson argue that today's urban "green" development opportunities require disinvested landscapes, and thus reinforce socioeconomic and racial inequalities. [Dis]investment in communities of color is among the subjects Brandi Thompson Summers discusses with Libby Viera-Bland in their broader conversation on Blackness and beauty that also touches on questions of representation, appropriation, and the racialized philosophical foundation upon which perceptions of beauty are built. And in an entirely different urban context across the pond, Vincent Baptist writes of design attempts to spatially organize the sex work industry within European cities, and how these spatial organizations privilege some and marginalize others.

In addition to cultural constructions of beauty we also turn to the science of beauty. Mechanical engineer Adrian Bejan, for example, argues that the definition of beauty is–biologically at least–fairly straightforward and tied to the physical parameters of sight. Once understood and reduced as such, beauty can then, according to Bejan, be mass produced. On the other hand, Jeffrey Blankenship and Jessica Hayes-Conroy downplay the role of the visual, arguing that beauty is visceral – tied to bodily need and physical comfort. For Sanda Iliescu, the question of beauty is both embodied and

Above: Hazy orange skies over San Francisco, California amidst wildfires north of the city on September 9, 2020.

visual. Through the discussion of her work *Poem Drawing: A Little Less Returned for Him Each Spring*, Iliescu explores the representation of landscapes and the capacity of drawing as a medium to represent the unfinished nature of landscapes as they change over time.

To bring these various threads back to landscape architecture *LA+* spoke with Elizabeth Meyer, the author of several well-known texts on contemporary landscape aesthetics. Meyer speaks to how she became interested in aesthetics, the significance of entanglement for landscape architecture, and where she finds beauty and aesthetic innovation in the field today.

Nicholas Holm concludes the issue by proposing the concept of "Natural Cosmetics" as a framework from which to understand and evaluate ideals of natural beauty. Returning in some ways to provocations set forth by Mariagrazia Portera at the beginning of the issue, Holm questions how we might open ourselves up to new aesthetics in a denatured world.

The motivation for this issue of *LA+* was a general sense that aesthetics are not adequately discussed in contemporary landscape architecture – that aesthetics are considered somehow secondary to other more pressing issues. I hope this collection shows that the two are not mutually exclusive: that issues are aesthetic and aesthetics are an issue.

Colin Curley
Issue Editor

THE AESTHETIC NICHE

MARIAGRAZIA PORTERA

Mariagrazia Portera is a research fellow in aesthetics at the Università di Firenze, Italy. Her areas of expertise and interest are the history of aesthetics (18th–19th century), the history of Darwinism, experimental aesthetics, and environmental and evolutionary aesthetics. Her work on epigenetics and evolutionary aesthetics has been published widely, including in *The British Journal of Aesthetics*.

✚ PHILOSOPHY, EVOLUTIONARY BIOLOGY, AESTHETICS

It is not obvious to answer the question "What is beauty?" Why do humans, from almost every culture in the world, invest so many resources in the beautification of their bodies, natural objects, and surroundings? Can we measure beauty? Are we biologically determined, as members of the species *Homo sapiens*, to find certain things invariably beautiful and others ugly?

Over the centuries, and within the framework of philosophical aesthetics, philosophers have championed an array of different hypotheses on beauty: some have argued that small, smooth, levigated forms are always and invariably beautiful (as opposed to angular and sharp ones, which are sublime; this is Edmund Burke's view in his 1757 *Inquiry into the Origin of Our Ideas of the Beautiful and the Sublime*). Some others have contended that beauty is no quality in things themselves; "it exists merely in the mind which contemplates them; and each mind perceives a different beauty."[1] Turning the spotlight onto empirical and experimental research on beauty, attempts have been made to

MULTISPECIES AESTHETICS IN TIMES OF ECOLOGICAL CRISIS

argue that there are universal standards of beauty concerning landscapes[2] and human bodies, that humans are predisposed to find symmetrical forms and contours aesthetically pleasant, and that they are innately attracted to other humans' faces (babies, in particular, tend to find symmetrical human faces most attractive).[3] Other scholars have traced beauty back to fluency, to the simplicity and smoothness of stimuli processing dynamics, so that the easier it is for humans to perceive and/or to conceptualize an object the more beautiful this object is judged to be.[4] There have also been researchers making a case for comparative approaches to beauty, under the premise that it might be that at least some human aesthetic standards apply not only or not exclusively to the human species but also to other nonhuman animal species, more or less phylogenetically close to us.[5]

A difficult point, when it comes to investigating the concept and standards of beauty, is whether it is possible to isolate biological-natural (allegedly universal) components of the beautiful (i.e., features or traits that are invariably perceived as beautiful by humans due to species-specific biological/cognitive/perceptual constraints) from cultural (relativist-historical) ones; and, if so, how these two components are or should be integrated.[6]

The concept of beauty is a *unitas multiplex* – a multifaceted, malleable, and multi-layered notion in which many elements intervene. Whenever humans experience something as beautiful (or whenever we have an aesthetic experience, since beauty represents only one of the several forms of aesthetic experience possible in the world) it involves at the same time perception, emotion, cognition, and imagination together with a self-reflecting activity on the part of the experiencing subject ("how does the experience I am having right now make me feel?"). This is why aesthetic experiences require time, and duration, to happen: although they certainly have to do with immediate (more or less perceptually pleasurable) appearances, they are not exhausted by them.

Research has shown that there is neither a single area of the brain nor a gene "responsible for all forms of beauty" that people are born with. Rather, the human aesthetic capacity—the capacity to engage in aesthetic experiences and to appreciate beauty—seems, on the one hand, to rely on the activation of an array of multiple neural circuits and brain areas and, on the other hand, to realize itself ontogenetically only if embedded in and scaffolded by suitable environments that ensure its development and transmittance. Even something so "simple" and apparently non-problematic as the allegedly universal attraction of human beings to symmetric stimuli has been called into question. Although "disciplines as diverse as biology, chemistry, physics, and psychological aesthetics regard symmetry as one of the most important principles in nature and as one of the most powerful determinants of beauty," write Austrian cognitive psychologist Helmut Leder and his collaborators in a recent paper, it seems that the level of expertise in aesthetics and the arts deeply affects the extent to which we appreciate symmetry.[7] People untrained in the visual arts do show the often-claimed preference for symmetry, but experts tend to disregard symmetry and show more consistent preferences for non-symmetrical stimuli.[8] Culture and experience matter.

It is also worth stressing that each of the objects with which we engage in aesthetic experiences is never "pure"—that is, neither purely natural nor purely cultural—but always the fruit of a co-construction of naturalness and "culturalness," even though not exclusively human-derived. This is obvious when we aesthetically appreciate the beauty of a human-made artifact, but it is also true (though perhaps somewhat less obvious) when we engage in aesthetic experiences with *natural* beauty, such as landscapes. The Tuscan landscape that surrounds me (I am writing this paper from Florence, Italy) is unanimously recognized as one of the most beautiful and aesthetically fascinating landscapes in Western Europe, celebrated by thousands of tourists and artists over centuries. Landscapes in Tuscany are, however, *nothing* purely natural (under the premise that we define the "naturalness" of an environmental object as "(in)dependence" – that the more or less an object's identity depends on human intervention and action, the more or less that object is natural or artificial/cultural, respectively[9]), but are rather the sedimentation of human and nonhuman natural-cultural transformative actions (I will come back to this point later), which *cumulatively* "make up" beauty.

A concept originally coined in the field of evolutionary biology—namely, the concept of the *niche* and the theory of niche construction—may help us better understand the interrelationship between natural-biological and cultural components of beauty and the intertwinement of human and nonhuman "aesthetic" actors. Through the lens of the niche, the historical and geographical variability of aesthetic standards and the human-nonhuman entanglement, also from an ecological-environmental perspective, come to the fore.[10]

The Concept of the Niche

Put forward by Harvard evolutionary biologist Richard Lewontin in a series of writings in the 1980s in which he argued for a transformative, non-passive relationship between organisms and their environment, the expression "niche construction" was formally introduced by John Odling-Smee. In his 2003 book *Niche Construction: The Neglected Process in Evolution*, Odling-Smee made a case for niche construction being the overlooked process in evolutionary theory, in the frame of a critical reassessment of some basic tenets of the Modern Synthesis of evolution. But what is a niche construction process?

A niche construction process is the process whereby organisms, through their activities and choices, modify their environment (niche), that is, the portion of territory in which they live and thrive, with expected consequences on the niches of other animals and plants. Through these environmental modifications, organisms generate a complex system of feedback loops that affect the selective pressures acting on them. Niche construction processes include the interaction of three basic factors: environmental modifications as a result of an organism's actions; a subsequent alteration of the (evolutionary) pressures acting on the niche-constructing organism (and, therefore, an alteration of the organism itself); and the transmission of these modifications over generations in the form of ecological inheritance.

Birds, termites, and ants with their nests, beavers with their dams, and honeybees with their hives are all examples, to various extents, of niche-constructing animals. For instance, let's say that a population of beavers sets up a dam that, by holding the water back, alters the flow of a river or stream so that a new (artificial?) stretch of water emerges. In this way, beavers mediately and indirectly (through their transformative actions on their environment) modify the environmental pressures acting on them in terms of food availability, shelter, protection from possible predators, and so on. But it is humans who are undoubtedly the most astonishing niche-constructing species in the animal kingdom: by constructing niches, *Homo sapiens* has changed the physiognomy of the entire planet – for better or for worse. Moreover, not only do humans physically construct their niche environments but they also culturally shape them.

Unlike "natural" niches such as the beavers' ones, a cultural niche is "that subset of niche construction that is the expression of culturally learned and transmitted knowledge (as opposed to individually learned or genetic information)."[11] In a cultural niche construction process, one or more culturally acquired traits (such as, for instance, the introduction of a new farming method) modify the environment in which organisms develop and species evolve – in other words, the environmental selective pressures exerted on them, thus generating a feedback action from the higher levels of culture to lower-level structures (genes, for example). It is widely acknowledged that cultural traits such as the advent of dairy farming have played a role in driving human biological evolution (in this specific example, the spread of the genes for lactose tolerance in certain human populations). Culture has the power to modify biology within the niche, which means, among other things, that our biological-natural make-up is not set in stone.

Darwin and the (Aesthetic) Niche Construction

While the first formalized articulation of the niche construction theory dates back no more than a couple of decades,[12] Charles Darwin had begun to explore its core concept at the end of the 19th century. The great Victorian was deeply fascinated by all aspects of transformative, non-passive relationships between organisms and their environments. What's more, Darwin seemed to be aware of an intriguing relationship between what would later come to be known as niche construction theory and the aesthetic domain.

In the last paragraph of his book *The Formation of Vegetable Mould, through the Action of Worms* (1881), while describing how earthworms construct their niche, Darwin writes:

> When we behold a wide, turf-covered expanse, we should remember that its smoothness, on *which so much of its beauty depends*, is mainly due to all the inequalities having been slowly levelled by worms. It is a marvellous reflection that the whole of the superficial mould over any such expanse has passed, and will again pass, every few years through the bodies of worms. The plough is one of the most ancient and most valuable of man's inventions; but long before he existed the land was in fact regularly ploughed, and still continues to be thus ploughed by earthworms. It may be doubted whether there are many other animals which have played so important a part in the history of the world, as have these lowly organized creatures.[13]

A thought-provoking link is drawn here between a niche-constructing species– earthworms–and the beauty of the English fields. Earthworms construct their niche through castings and excretions, actively shaping the English landscape, leveling its rough irregularities and slowly transforming them into smooth surfaces. In doing so, they contribute to the construction of what Darwin, as a 19th-century English gentleman, finds beautiful (smooth) in the English countryside. Is this a natural beauty, or not? And what does "natural" mean (as opposed to "cultural"), in the context of a niche construction process?

Three further things should be stressed, as to the relevance of Darwin's reflections to aesthetics. First, in Darwin's view (human) beauty is not immutable or fixed, but rather the outcome of processes of transformation of the environment (understood in a dynamic sense) in which synergy between nonhuman organic and inorganic components is at work – in this case, synergy between the digestive activity of earthworms and the

1 This is, famously, David Hume's empiricist concept of beauty. See David Hume, "Of the Standard of Taste," in *Four Dissertations* (A. Millar, 1757).

2 Ecologists G. H. Orians and J. H. Hervageen championed these ideas in "Evolved Responses to Landscapes," in Jerome H. Barkow, Leda Cosmides & John Tooby (eds), *The Adapted Mind* (Oxford University Press, 1992), 555–79.

3 See, for this, Gillian Rhodes, et al., "Are Average and Symmetric Faces Attractive to Infants? Discrimination and looking preferences" *Perception* 31 (2002): 315–21.

4 The theory of fluency, applied to aesthetics, is described in Rolf Reber, Norbet Schwarz & Piotr Winkielman, "Processing Fluency and Aesthetic Pleasure: Is beauty in the perceiver's processing experience? *Personality and Social Psychology Review* 8, no. 4 (2004): 364–82.

5 I have discussed pitfalls and promises of a comparative research program in aesthetics in the paper: M. Portera, "Animal Aesthetics? Promises and Challenges of a Comparative Research Programme in Aesthetics" in Martino Rossi Monti & Davor Pecnjak, *What is Beauty? A Multidisciplinary Approach to Aesthetic Experience* (Cambridge Publishing Scholars, 2020), 60–80.

6 See for example Jan Verpooten & Siegfried Dewitte, "The Conundrum of Modern Art: Prestige-Driven Coevolutionary Aesthetics Trumps Evolutionary Aesthetics among Art Experts," *Human Nature* 28 (2017): 16–38.

7 See Helmut Leder, et al., "Symmetry Is Not a Universal Law of Beauty," *Empirical Studies of the Arts* 37, no. 1 (2019), 104–14.

8 Ibid.

9 I take this definition of natural/artificial from the brilliant paper by Elena Casetta, "Making Sense of Nature Conservation After the End of Nature," *History and Philosophy of the Life Sciences* 42, no. 18 (2020).

10 I have discussed the notion of the niche in two earlier papers and some sections of the present paper are taken, with modifications, from these two previous publications: Mariagrazia Portera, "Why Do Human Perceptions of Beauty Change? The Construction of the Aesthetic Niche, in Molding the Planet: Human Niche Construction at Work," *RCC Perspectives: Transformations in Environment and Society*, no. 5 (2016): 41–47; Mariagrazia Portera, "Babies Rule! Niches, Scaffoldings, and the Development of an Aesthetic Capacity in Humans," *The British Journal of Aesthetics* 60, no. 3 (2020): 299–314.

11 I am referring to Kevin N. Laland & Michael J. O'Brien, "Cultural Niche Construction: An Introduction," *Biological Theory* 6, no. 3 (2012): 191–202.

12 F. John Odling-Smee, Kevin N. Laland & Marcus W. Feldman, *Niche Construction: The Neglected Process in Evolution* (Princeton University Press, 2003).

13 Charles R. Darwin, *The Formation of Vegetable Mould, through the Action of Worms, with Observations on Their Habits* (John Murray, 1881), 313 (my emphasis).

14 Charles R. Darwin, *The Descent of Man, and Selection in Relation to Sex* (John Murray, 1871).

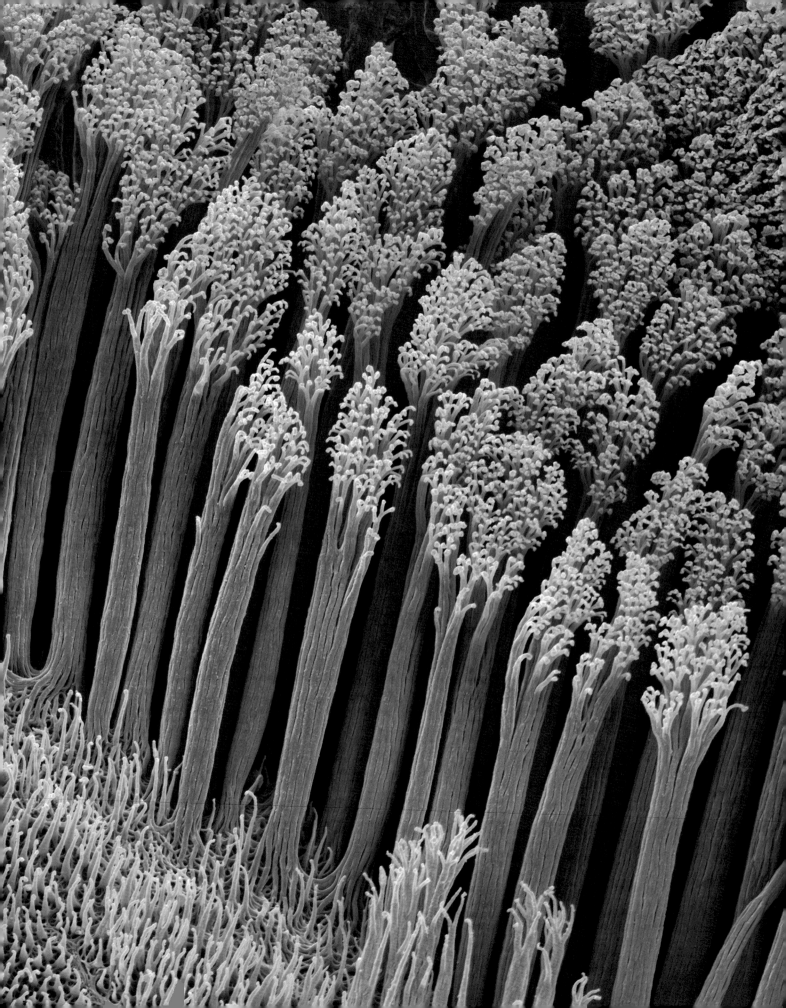

characteristics of the soil in the English countryside. As Darwin writes in his *The Descent of Man*, "It is certainly not true that there is in the mind of man any universal standard of beauty with respect to the human body. It is, however, possible that certain tastes may in the course of time become inherited...and if so, each race would possess its own innate ideal standard of beauty."[14] Although the English naturalist is here referring specifically to the beauty of the human body, his hypotheses may easily be extended to the concept of beauty as a whole: nothing fixed or immutable, but rather a transformative and malleable concept. Second, Darwin ironically points here to the fact that even what human beings generally regard as one of the highest results of their cultural evolution (the idea of beauty, and the capacity to have aesthetic experiences) actually relies on the ordinary, unpretentious, even modest (digestive) activity of the most elementary nonhuman life forms, i.e., earthworms. Third, there is according to Darwin no opposition, but rather continuity between nature and culture, also concerning aesthetic standards. This latter point comes clearly to the fore if we consider the closing sentences of the abovementioned passage, in which Darwin draws an intriguing analogy between the plough, as one of the most valuable human cultural inventions, and the action of earthworms: "long before [the plough] existed the land was in fact regularly ploughed, and still continues to be thus ploughed by earthworms." What is beauty, then? Something the standards of which may change, something that—in Darwin's view—results from the entanglement of humans and nonhumans within their intertwined niches. Something concerning which the classical nature/culture dichotomy seems to lose its significance.

Niche Construction in Contemporary Aesthetics

There has recently been growing interest in the concept of the niche, particularly within the field of aesthetics and the arts. I restrict myself to a couple of examples, both referring to scholars working on the boundaries between aesthetics, evolutionary biology, and the cognitive sciences. The first example comes from Stephen Davies's research, which has substantially contributed over the last two decades to reframing the debate in evolutionary aesthetics. Moving from a critical reassessment of the evolutionary aesthetics state-of-the-art, Davies, in his book *The Artful Species*,[15] makes a convincing case for rejecting the traditional triadic way of interpreting the evolutionary origin of the aesthetic and of the human capacity to appreciate beauty: that is, the aesthetic in humans is either an adaptation (directly molded and shaped by natural selection), a byproduct of other adaptations, or an exaptation (i.e., a functional shift). As he puts it, "there may be no clear answer to the question framed as one about whether the arts [or the human capacity to appreciate beauty] are adaptations or by-product, or whether they are primarily biological or cultural. Culture affects our evolved biology, our biology limits what is culturally possible, and the two are in constant interaction, with feedback in both directions. Above all, we are niche-constructing species."[16] In this sense,

instead of discussing which of the three above-mentioned options might better suit the aesthetic, Davies suggests that we look at how we (and our ancestors before us) construct and populate our *aesthetic niches*.[17]

With different aims than Davies's ones, the notion of the niche has also been discussed by Richard A. Richards, who adopts the niche-perspective to address issues of normativity.[18] Here are, in short, the main points of his argument. Human beings construct different niches (in other words, different environments, both in the sense of physical spaces and of the systems of norms, traditions, and conventions that regulate the activity) for different types of aesthetic activity, and not all individuals interact in all niches in the same way. "The people who interact in the dance niches, for instance, are typically not the same people who interact in the visual art or museum niches. And the people who interact within the dance subniches, ballet for instance, are typically not the same people who interact within the modern dance, Argentine tango, ballroom or hip-hop niches." Aesthetic niches change over time. Some of them are nested into each other, others are totally unrelated; and totally unrelated niches may enter into conflict. Richards puts forward a distinction between a niche-dependent normativity (the conventional norms in use within a particular environment, the product of cognitive and pedagogical technologies) and a niche-independent normativity, "based on the evolved neuropsychology, tendencies, and preferences of individuals." These concepts reflect a "cultural niche" normativity and a "biological niche" normativity. Given the large number of cultural aesthetic niches that humans incessantly construct and into which they are transversally embedded, it is very unlikely, Richards argues, that the niche-dependent stream of normativity coincides exactly with the niche-independent. Therefore, universal norms are very unlikely in aesthetics. In this sense—and pretty much along the lines of Darwin's original argument in his book on earthworms—the niche perspective can help us understand why standards of beauty are never given once and for all, but rather can change, vary, and be transformed.

Drawing on recent research developments in evolutionary biology, developmental psychology, and cognitive sciences, I have adopted the concept of the niche to shed some light on the development and functioning of the aesthetic capacity in humans and its trans-generational transmission. More specifically, I have argued that the human aesthetic capacity—understood as the capacity, involving perceptual, cognitive, and emotional processes to enter into a pleasurable relation with objects, artworks, natural phenomena, or other people—relies on constructed environmental resources (that is, on a niche) for its emergence and its ontogenetic development. Would a human being develop an aesthetic capacity if deprived of a suitably scaffolded aesthetic niche (including inter-individual and environmental transactions)? No, she would not. The built niche, as a developmental system including genetic, epigenetic, social, cultural, and physical constituents (every one of which is affected by the activities of the others) allows the trait–the aesthetic capacity and the capacity to appreciate beauty–to emerge and be transmitted. It "makes" the trait. In this sense, the perspective of the niche is crucial in aesthetics. Aesthetic niches are built, shared, constructed, molded, and renovated; as much as our aesthetic niches, also our standard of beauty and the idea itself of what beauty is may change and *does* change over time.

Entanglements

The question of the niche in its implications for aesthetics can be tackled from several points of view, from normativity to the idea of the historicity of beauty, from the nature/culture dichotomy to the emergence of the aesthetic (as a human capacity) within the developmental niche.

Here I would like to focus on a specific aspect of the niche dynamics, that is, the "entanglement" of *human/nonhuman* niches, their being deeply "nested" one within another in a multispecies pyramid structure, and the relevance of this idea to our understanding of beauty – or, more generally, of aesthetic experiences. One intriguing aspect of the (aesthetic) niche dynamics highlighted by Charles Darwin in his piece on earthworms is that human standards of beauty might be said to rely on the cooperation of *multiple actors*, both human and nonhuman, for their emergence and relative stabilization. I am interested in bringing to the fore the potential of this idea for ecological thinking. To develop my point, I shall start by laying some stress on the notion of the niche against the background of today's hotly debated concept of the "Anthropocene."

In 2001, Nobel prize-winning chemist Paul Crutzen introduced the term Anthropocene (in place of "Holocene") to characterize the current geological epoch, arguing that human niche-constructing activities and human-induced changes in Earth's ecosystems have today reached such a magnitude that we could speak of a new age in Earth's history, "the Age of Man." The current ecological crisis is just one of the multiple pieces of evidence of *Homo sapiens'* extensive and global impact on the Earth geology, and on the Earth as a whole, in the Anthropocene.

Since 2001, the concept of the Anthropocene has been taken up by a wide number of scholars from fields as different as geology, ecology, literary studies, eco-philosophy, sociology, and the arts. This increasing popularity, however, has gone hand in hand with growing criticisms, the most representative of which might be summed up as follows. It is not *Homo sapiens* per se–as the label "The Age of Man – Anthropocene" seems to suggest–that is responsible for the current ecological crisis, it is the late-capitalist lifestyle that continues to squander Earth's resources as if they were unlimited (including nonhuman animals, marginalized people, and any other forms of life), and a relatively small portion of the global population (living in late-capitalist countries) that is shortsightedly responsible for almost the whole global ecological disaster. American philosopher Donna Haraway, for instance, has extensively criticized the notion of the Anthropocene challenging its focus on humanity as such (*anthropos*), and has suggested that it would be more accurate to speak of the "Capitalocene."

In her 2016 essay "Tentacular Thinking," Haraway put forward a third way (besides "Anthropocene" and "Capitalocene") to think about the interrelations of humans and nonhumans in the context of today's environmental catastrophe: the notion of the Chthulucene. While Anthropocene and Capitalocene seem both, she argues, "to lend themselves too readily to cynicism, defeatism, and self-certain and self-fulfilling predictions, like the 'game over, too late' discourse I hear all around me these days, in both experts and popular discourses,"[19] with the term "Chthulucene" the focus is on "ongoing multispecies stories and practices of becoming…in precarious time, in which the world is not finished and the sky has not fallen – yet."[20] In the Chthulucene, humans, although undoubtedly the species with the greatest responsibility toward the global environment, are recognized as only one of the actors involved in the transformation of the planet. *Homo sapiens* is deeply interwoven with all other organic and inorganic components of the Earth, and profoundly embedded in multispecies bonds. As already foreseen by Darwin with specific regard to the human standards of beauty and to aesthetic experiences, there is an entanglement of species at work in nature, so that even what looks like the purest and most "human" of the categories–beauty–is indeed the result of a human/nonhuman unintentional cooperation. In other words, even what looks like the "most exclusively human" of the niches is, in fact, a nest of interwoven niches.

In *Staying with the Trouble*, Haraway's poetic imaginary about the Chthulucene is channeled into the invention of fantastic stories of symbiotic interactions. Haraway carries out a sort of experiment of creative writing in which her hybridized creative imagination becomes the most promising reservoir for some possible hope in times of ecological disaster. The fantastic stories that conclude *Staying with the Trouble* describe multispecies niches in which humans intentionally hybridize with endangered nonhuman species (butterflies, fishes, birds, amphibians) to increase their mutual chances of survival. What results from such hybrid niches are new forms of life, endowed with a weird, eerie, *un*-usual beauty.

Haraway imagines that, in the midst of the ecological crisis, hundreds of people in West Virginia decide to make a last, desperate effort to give themselves and the other nonhuman species at risk of extinction a chance to survive the environmental destruction. They build new settlements and inaugurate new human/nonhuman communities, called the "Communities of Compost," and their members "the Compostists." Within these communities, new human babies are bonded with animal symbionts; Camille 1 is one of the first among these little hybrids. Haraway writes:

> People knew it would not be simple to learn to live collectively in intimate and worldly caretaking symbiosis with another animal as a practice of repairing damaged places and making flourishing multispecies futures. Camille 1 was born among a small group of five children, and was the only youngster linked to an insect. Other children in this first cohort became symbionts with fish (American eel, *Anguilla rostrata*), birds (American kestrel, *Falco sparverius*), crustaceans (the Big Sandy crayfish, *Cambarus veteranus*), and amphibians (streamside salamander, *Ambystoma barbouri*).[21]

What do these hybrids look like? Do they look beautiful, or instead terrifying or sublime? What kind of emotional response do they elicit? As known, a hybrid in biology is the offspring of plants or animals of different varieties or species; the word, coming from Latin *hybrida*, is probably related to the Greek *hybris*, meaning "insolence towards the gods; outrage." What kind of beauty are these "insolent" hybrids endowed with? In Primo Levi's short story "Angelic Butterfly," hybrids are presented as the result of a horrifying experiment run by Nazi professor Leeb, who in an excess of hubris tries to bring humans to their most perfect level of development, transforming them into winged creatures like angels or butterflies.[22] A dramatic proof of insolence toward God or, to the contrary, the last, desperate effort to fly away from the horror of Nazi Germany? What are hybrids for?

It might even be that, in the Anthropocene, we need once and for all to abandon the notion of beauty as a peace-inducing, comforting, pleasurable experience and be attuned instead to radically new, thought-provoking forms of aesthetic experiences, ethically connoted, for which we do not have a suitable name yet and the multiple possibilities of which are still to be explored. "People knew it would not be simple to learn to live collectively in intimate and worldly caretaking symbiosis with another animal as a practice of repairing damaged places and making flourishing multispecies futures," Haraway writes. Although not simple, to learn a multispecies theory and practice of aesthetic experience within our interwoven human/nonhuman niches seems to be, today, the only possible strategy to *stay with the trouble* and at the same time try to repair (our own) environmental damages. The Anthropocene is, in the end, very much an aesthetic project.

15 Stephen Davies, *The Artful Species: Aesthetics, Art, and Evolution* (Oxford University Press, 2012).

16 Stephen Davies, "Evolution, Aesthetics, and Art: An Overview," in Richard Joyce (ed.), *The Routledge Handbook of Evolution and Philosophy* (Routledge, 2018), 359–71, 368.

17 See Richard Menary, "The Aesthetic Niche," *British Journal of Aesthetics* 54, no. 4 (2014): 471–75.

18 Richard A. Richards, "Engineered Niches and Naturalized Aesthetics," *The Journal of Aesthetics and Art Criticism* 75 (2017): 465–77.

19 Donna Haraway, "Tentacular Thinking: Anthropocene, Capitalocene, Chthulucene," *E-flux Journal 75* (September 2016), https://www.e-flux.com/journal/75/67125/tentacular-thinking-anthropocene-capitalocene-chthulucene/.

20 Ibid.

21 Donna Haraway, *Staying with the Trouble: Making Kin in the Chthulucene* (Duke University Press, 2016), 146.

22 Primo Levi, "Angelic Butterfly," in *The Sixth Day and Other Tales* (Michael Joseph, 1990), 18–26.

Previous: Microscopic image of gecko lizard toe hairs.

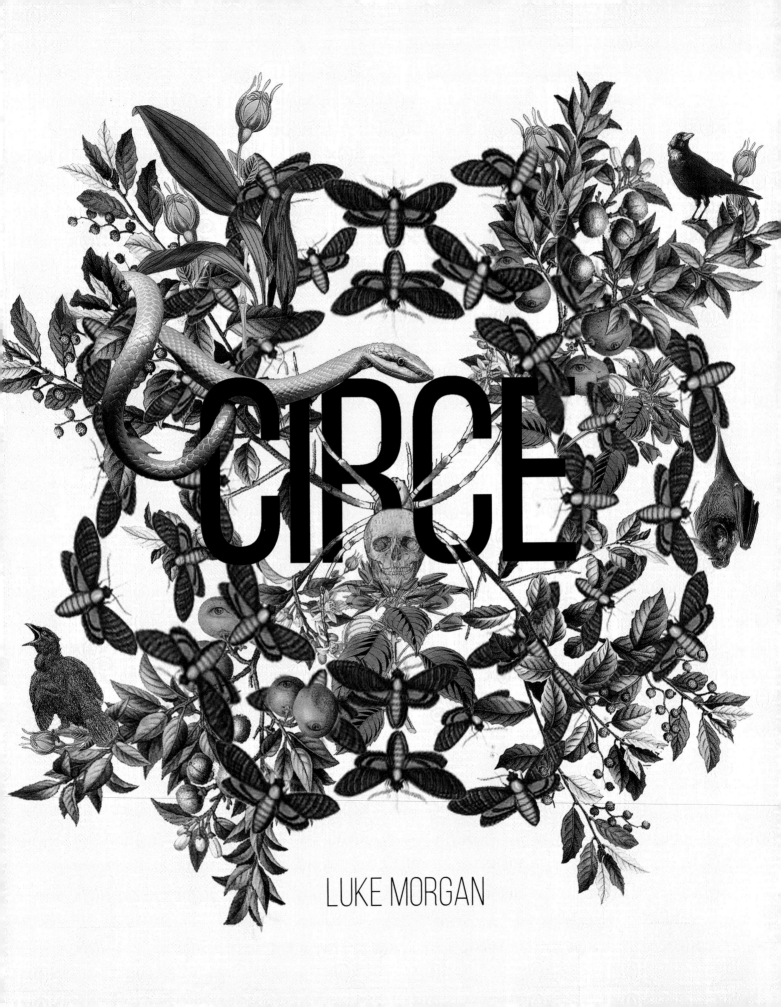

CIRCE

LUKE MORGAN

COUNTER-NARRATIVES OF BEAUTY IN RENAISSANCE LANDSCAPE DESIGN

Luke Morgan is professor of art history and theory at Monash University and an Australian Research Council Future Fellow. He is also a fellow of the Australian Academy of the Humanities. His books include *Nature as Model: Salomon de Caus and Early Seventeenth-Century Landscape Design* (2006), and *The Monster in the Garden: The Grotesque and the Gigantic in Renaissance Landscape Design* (2016), both published by The University of Pennsylvania Press.

+ ART HISTORY, LITERATURE, AESTHETICS

Dosso Dossi's painting *Circe and Her Lovers in a Landscape* (c. 1525) depicts the mythical Greek enchantress in a wood accompanied by animals and birds. She is portrayed nude except for the wreath of flowers that crowns her long blonde hair and the green drapery that covers her left leg. In her hands she holds a large stone tablet inscribed with characters. A book of spells is depicted at her feet, open to a page containing an annotated diagram of concentric circles with, at its center, a pentagram.

Although in the earliest source of the myth, Homer's *Odyssey*, Circe is straightforwardly described as beautiful, the beauty of her 16th-century descendants is ultimately revealed to be a dangerous illusion.[1] For example, in the epic poem *Orlando Furioso* (1516) by Dossi's Ferrarese compatriot and friend Ludovico Ariosto, Ruggiero's initial impression of the witch Alcina is that she is "so beautifully modelled, no painter, however much he applied himself, could have achieved anything more perfect."[2] Dossi's depiction of Circe recalls Ariosto's detailed description of Alcina's physical perfection, as if the painter had consciously responded to the poet's challenge.[3] Circe, like Alcina, has "long blonde tresses," a brow "like polished ivory," a "snow-white" neck, "milky" breasts, and "lily-white" hands that are "slender and tapering."[4] However, when Ruggiero finally sees Alcina clearly with the help of a magic ring, he realizes that her

> beauty was in every detail an imposture: it was wholly fraudulent – nothing, from her soles up to her tresses, was natural to her...in place of the beauty he had just parted from, he was confronted with a woman so hideous that her equal for sheer ugliness and decrepitude could be found nowhere on earth. She was whey-faced, wrinkled, and hollow-cheeked; her hair was white and sparse; she was not four feet high; the last tooth had dropped out of her jaw; she had lived longer than anyone on earth, longer than Hecuba or the Cumaean Sibyl. But she made such use of arts unknown in our day that she could pass for young and fair. Young and fair she made herself by artifice, and deceived many as she deceived Ruggiero.[5]

The landscape inhabited by Alcina is just as fraudulent as her beauty. Inevitably, tiring of her lovers (numbering more than 1,000), she "transforms them, every one, planting them here and there in the fertile soil, changing one into a fir-tree, another into an olive, another into a palm or cedar...yet others the proud enchantress changes into liquid springs, or into beasts, just as it suits her."[6] Through her necromantic arts, therefore, Alcina transforms herself and her environment.

Ariosto's probable influence on Dossi suggests that the pastoral veneer of the painting, with its Giorgionesque landscape and docile animals, should be understood as concealing the violent acts of transformation that have ushered this apparent idyll into existence. Nothing in the image is as it seems: Circe's beauty is an illusion; the animals are her former lovers, once human but now reduced to beasts; and even the tranquil landscape environment of the scene is an artificial creation. This is, in short, a false paradise.

Christopher S. Wood has argued that for Dossi, Circe was "a textual and iconographic framework for addressing the complex psychological problems of the delusion of the senses, imagination, sexual enchantment, and beauty."[7] In Dossi's painting and the poems that inspired it, the landscape setting both extends the enchantress's artificial persona into the surrounding environment and serves as the principal site of her sorcery and its psychological effects. Delusion, imagination, enchantment (sexual or otherwise) and beauty are also key themes in the experience and reception of real landscapes during the 16th and early 17th centuries.

Gardens deluded the beholder in multiple ways: from fountains, grottoes, and other structures that deliberately blurred the boundaries between art and nature to the seemingly sentient statues of hydraulically powered automated tableaux. Imagination or *fantasia*, to use a term from the theoretical literature of 16th-century art, is one of the sources of the hybrid and grotesque figures of the Renaissance garden.[8] Enchantment is, similarly, the frequently attested condition of the garden visitor of the period. The Elizabethan writer Thomas Nashe's description of the garden of an Italian merchant in which mechanical birds ("bodies without souls") occupy the metal boughs of a "conspiracy of pine trees" is representative. According to him: "every man there present renounced conjectures of art and said it was done by enchantment."[9]

Wood's last "problem"–beauty–is a deeply ambivalent concept in representations of Circe and her descendants in landscape settings. This article proposes that the literary figure of the enchantress in the garden problematizes a number of received ideas about the connotations of beauty in Renaissance landscape design. The Circean garden, created through necromancy, is a beautiful but perilous place where art suppresses and supersedes nature. "Magic art here wields / a power so great that even Nature yields," as the poet Torquato Tasso wrote of the enchantress Armida's bower in *Gerusalemme Liberata* (1581).[10] In these fictional landscapes, beauty is a negative principle – a synonym for unnatural magic that in every case causes the self-deluded hero to languish in what Tasso evocatively describes as a "drunken dream / of pampered ease in pleasure's paradise."[11] Notably, this idea of the garden as a false paradise–the beauty of which is morally suspect–also informed the responses of 16th- and 17th-century visitors to real landscapes.

The Enchantress in the Garden

In *The Odyssey*, Homer links Circe's magical powers to her knowledge of the effects of rare plants and herbs (later cultivated in gardens of simples or herb gardens and, during the Renaissance, in botanic gardens), and their usage in drugs (*pharmaka*). At the very beginning of the Circe myth, therefore, the enchantress's powers are derived from her expert knowledge of pharmacopoeia, or of the secrets of nature, but she remains a comparatively benign figure.

It is only in later Roman literature that Circe is portrayed as a seductive witch. The most influential characterization of Circe in this guise is that of Ovid, who was widely read during the Renaissance. In Book 14 of *Metamorphoses*, Circe appears

three times. In each case, Ovid emphasizes her sexual desire[12] for, consecutively, Glaucus, Ulysses [Odysseus], and Picus. Circe's power to transform not only men but whole landscapes is introduced in the last episode. When Picus's men threaten Circe, she responds by sprinkling her "noxious drugs and poisonous juices" and by howling incantations.

> Then from the ground there sprang up a miraculous grove, the earth gave a groan, and the neighbouring trees grew pale. The grass which Circe had sprinkled was wet with drops like blood, the stones seemed to utter hoarse rumblings, dogs barked, the earth crawled with black snakes, and shadowy ghosts flitted noiselessly here and there. The band of huntsmen, dismayed by these horrors, trembled with fear. Then, as they gasped in wonder and terror, Circe touched their faces with her magic wand, and at its touch the young men were transformed into wild beasts of various kinds. Not one of them retained his own form.[13]

Although Circe turns the woods of Latium into a *locus horridus* [fearful place], her falsification of nature provides a precedent for the transformative magic of the enchantresses of Renaissance poetry.

Ariosto's account of Alcina's metamorphosis of her lovers, not just into animals as in Ovid, but into trees, plants, and topographical features has already been mentioned. Another example of transformation at the scale of landscape is provided by Armida's castle in *Gerusalemme Liberata*, which is located on the site of Sodom and Gomorrah in the Dead Sea: "a tepid, sulphurous sty, / a sterile lake. All shores its slow waves drench / exude through thickening air a dreadful stench." "[B]y uncanny art," however, Armida's realm is "fair and smiles in every part."[14] The enchantress conjures a locus amoenus [pleasant place] in the midst of the hellish landscape, which is the legacy of corruption and sin. Similarly, in the English Renaissance poem *The Faerie Queene* [1590], which owes much to Ariosto and Tasso, the enchantress Acrasia's Bower of Bliss seems equally idyllic but, as Edward Spenser writes, it is revealed to be the "fowlest place" guarded by men who have been transformed into raging wild beasts.[15]

Alcina, Armida, and Acrasia are, like Ovid's Circe, pitiless sorceresses, whose beauty and paradisiacal landscape realms are seductive illusions. In each case, the figure of the enchantress is also a kind of abstraction, embodying a moral lesson. Her role is to entrap the hero and distract him from his true path. She thus encapsulates male fears about the perils of submission to temptation, which include indulgence in sensual pleasure at the expense of higher thought and, ultimately, the loss of identity.

Unnatural Nature

Circe and her Renaissance descendants all inhabit garden or landscape environments. In each case, the beauty of the setting is inextricably linked to the dangerous woman at its center.[16] One potential implication of this association is that to submit to the garden's delights is as irrational as submission to Circe herself. Judith Yarnall has drawn attention to other early modern genres, besides poetry, in which Circe's transformation of men into beasts is presented as a metaphorical representation of the consequences of male lust and sexual obsession. Circe appears, for example, in the illustrations of many emblem books. In Andreas Alciati's *Emblemata*, which was first published in 1531 and saw many subsequent editions, she is depicted as a prostitute. The last lines of the text beneath Emblem LXXVI of the 1621 Padua edition of the *Emblemata*, in which Circe stands on the shore of her island towering over the figures of the men in their boat, read "whoever loves her has lost his mind's reason."[17]

The negative image of the garden as a place in which rationality and morality are corrupted by beauty and pleasure becomes a recurring idea in 16th-century poetry from *Orlando furioso* to *The Faerie Queene*. Ruggiero, for example, still under Alcina's spell, is depicted by Ariosto, "enjoying the freshness and peace of the morning beside a delightful stream which flowed down a hillside towards a pleasant, limpid lake."[18] Ruggiero's appearance is a correlative of his idealized environment: "The delicious softness of his dress suggested sloth and sensuality." Handsomely attired in fine silk, gold, and pearls, his hair "saturated in perfumes," nonetheless, "[a]ll about him was sickly, all but his name; the rest was but corruption and decay. Thus was Ruggiero discovered, thus changed from his true self by sorcery."[19] Ruggiero's enslavement by and absorption in his false beloved and her equally false paradise has emasculated him: "his two arms, hitherto so virile, were now each clasped by a lustrous bangle... his every gesture was mincing, as though he were accustomed to waiting on ladies in Valencia."[20] The effete "shackles which had been forced upon him by sorcery" have distracted him from his Christian mission.[21]

There is a similar association of designed landscape and the changed appearance and behavior of the male victim in *Gerusalemme liberata*. Within Armida's mountaintop fastness is

> [a] garden [that] lies amidst this daunting maze / whose every leaf breathes Love upon that ground. / Embowered there in fresh and verdant grass / you'll find the knight reclining with his lass [Armida]." The Sage of Ascalon (a practitioner of natural magic rather than the demonic magic wielded by Armida) who provides this information then instructs the knight Rinaldo's men to "lift the diamond shield, / that I shall give you, right before his [Rinaldo's] eyes, / that in it he may see his face revealed / and the effeminate garb in which he lies; / and at that sight, shame and disdain may start / to chase unworthy love out of his heart.[22]

Through beneficent magic (a ring and a shield), both Ruggiero and Rinaldo are released from their enchantment. They immediately regain their wits, or self-identities, and their moral purposes. In *Orlando furioso*, Alcina's true hideousness is revealed. In *Gerusalemme liberata*, the previously idyllic landscape fades like "dreams by a sick man" leaving behind only "the mountains and the frosts that nature made."[23] The seductive beauty of the enchantress and the concomitant pleasures of her bower, which are as much a part of her allure as her physical beauty, are shown to be phantasms.

The association of enchantress and garden in a composite image of corruption and depravity is also common in late 16th-century English poetry.[24] Christine Coch has argued that the reappearance and repetition of the motif of the dangerous woman in the garden was in part the result of an "ambivalence toward sensual pleasure [that] was conventionally schematized in gendered form."[25] *The Faerie Queene* is the most sophisticated meditation of the period on this theme. Spenser portrays the young knight Verdant as an impotent devotee of the enchantress, recalling Ruggiero and Rinaldo, having literally removed and hung up his armor and weapons. Spenser writes: "Ne for them, ne for honour cared hee, / Ne ought, that did to his aduauncement tend, / But in lewd loues, and wastfull luxuree, / His dayes, his goods, his bodie did he spende: / O horrible enchantment, that him so did blend."[26]

Verdant is enslaved by Acrasia's beauty and desirability, underlining Coch's point about the misogynistic character of the period's distrust of sensual pleasure. Spenser compares her "alabaster skin," "snowy breast," and "faire eyes sweet smyling in delight" to Arachne's web.[27] The sensual pleasures of Acrasia's Bower of Bliss are also described in gendered terms: "Wherewith her mother Art, as halfe in scorne / Of niggard Nature, like a pompous bride / Did decke her, and too lauishly adorne, / When forth from virgin bowre she comes in th'early morne."[28]

Spenser's comparison of Acrasia's garden to a "pompous bride" who is "too lavishly" adorned by art is reflective of the greater anxiety in English Renaissance literature

1 Homer, *The Odyssey*, rev. trans. D. C. H. Rieu (Penguin, 2003), 128.

2 Ludovico Ariosto, *Orlando Furioso*, trans. Guido Waldman (Oxford University Press, 2008), 61.

3 Ariosto's passage (Canto 7) is probably the most famous description of female beauty in the early 16th century. This point is from Giancarlo Fiorenza, "Studies in Dosso Dossi's Pictorial Language: Painting and Humanist Culture in Ferrara under Duke Alfonso I d'Este," PhD diss., The Johns Hopkins University (2000), 272.

4 Ariosto, *Orlando Furioso*, 61.

5 Ibid., 68–69.

6 Ibid., 56.

7 Christopher S. Wood, "Countermagical Combinations by Dosso Dossi," *RES: Anthropology and Aesthetics*, no. 49/50 (2006): 163.

8 On fantasia in 16th-century art theory, see David Summers, *Michelangelo and the Language of Art* (Princeton University Press, 1981), 103ff. On the hybrid and grotesque figures of the Renaissance garden, see my *The Monster in the Garden: The Grotesque and the Gigantic in Renaissance Landscape Design* (University of Pennsylvania Press, 2016).

9 Thomas Nashe, *The Unfortunate Traveller*, in *An Anthology of Elizabethan Prose Fiction*, ed. Paul Salzman (Oxford University Press, 1987), 272. Note that this is a fictional evocation of real Italian gardens.

10 Torquato Tasso, *The Liberation of Jerusalem*, trans. Max Wickert (Oxford University Press, 2009), 281.

11 Ibid., 291.

12 Ovid, *Metamorphoses*, trans. Mary M. Innes (Penguin, 1955), 311.

13 Ibid., 322.

14 Tasso, *Liberation of Jerusalem*, 195.

15 Edward Spenser, *The Faerie Queene* (Penguin, 1987), 381–82.

16 See A. Bartlett Giamatti, *The Earthly Paradise and the Renaissance Epic* (Princeton University Press, 1969), 153, on *Orlando Furioso*: "the false garden of Alcina is the best symbol of Alcina."

17 The title of the emblem is *Cavendum a meretricibus* ("Beware of Prostitutes"). See Judith Yarnall, *Transformations of Circe: The History of an Enchantress* (University of Illinois Press, 1994), 106.

18 Ariosto, *Orlando Furioso*, 66.

19 Ibid.

20 Ibid.

21 Ibid., 68.

22 Tasso, *The Liberation of Jerusalem*, 271.

23 Ibid, 300.

24 For the general association of women with gardens, see Christine Coch, "The Woman in the Garden: [En]gendering Pleasure in Late Elizabethan Poetry," *English Literary Renaissance* 39: 1 (Winter 2009): 97–127.

25 Ibid., 99.

26 Spenser, *Fairie Queene*, 381.

27 Ibid., 380.

about the relationship between art and nature within gardens, bowers, and other designed landscapes. This is especially true of the enchanted gardens of poetry, but concerns about the usurpation of nature by art are also encountered in descriptions of real landscapes and often attributed to Italian influence. John Earle, whose eulogistic poem about the garden of Merton College in Oxford, "Hortus Mertonensis" (1620), is also a diatribe against the "insolent address of art" in the "godless gardens which in vain / Th'italians for their heaven feign' provides an example."[29]

Contemporary methods of grafting provoked especially vitriolic critiques of the interference in nature for horticultural or aesthetic benefits. Andrew Marvell was highly critical of the practice in his poem "The Mower Against Gardens" (c. 1650). He regarded the gardens of his period as artificial impositions on "plain and pure" nature. Within the "dead and standing pool of air" of the garden, "No Plant now knew the Stock from which it came," thanks to the gardener who "grafts upon the wild the tame: / That the uncertain and adulterate fruit / Might put the palate in dispute." He was equally scornful of the garden's sculptural ornaments: "Tis all enforced, the fountain and the grot; / While the sweet Fields do lie forgot."[30]

Critics of grafting objected to the mixing of genera to produce new hybrids, or what Giambattista Della Porta in his widely read book *Magia Naturalis* (1558) called "copulation."[31] For Della Porta, copulation referred to the union or fusion of opposed or disparate entities, including plants.[32] In Renaissance landscape design as much as in architectural discourse, copulation has an analogue in the aesthetic concept of *mescolanza* (mixture).[33] For example, in his description of a grotto in a garden near the Trevi Fountain in Rome, the philologist Claudio Tolomei used the word *mescolando* ("mixing" or "mingling"). Tolomei writes that: "mingling [*mescolando*] art with nature, one does not know how to discern whether it is a work of the former or the latter; on the contrary, now it seems to be a natural artifice, then an artificial nature."[34] In his formulation, art and nature mingle in the creation of a grotto that defeats categorization.

These points about grafting, copulation, and *mescolanza* again lead back to the figure of the enchantress in the garden. The 16th-century mythographer Natalis Comes portrays Circe as both a mixture herself and as the medium through which the elements are manipulated and combined to engender new forms and beings.[35] Circe, he writes, presides over sex and childbirth because "lust is made in animals out of moisture and heat," the same elements of which she is herself constituted.[36] Della Porta's notion of "copulation" thus has a pseudo-ancient lineage.[37] The idea is appropriated by George Sandys in his English translation of Ovid's *Metamorphoses* (1621): "Circe is so-called of mixing, because the mixture of the elements is necessary in generation which cannot be performed but by the motion of the sun: Persis, or moisture supplying the place of the female, and the Sun of the male, which gives forme to the matter: wherefore that commixtion in generation is properly Circe, the issue of these parents."[38]

Conclusion: Circe as a Symbolic Figure

Circe thus personifies and even literally embodies a key principle of the early modern garden: *mescolanza*. Through her magic arts, men are transformed into beasts, forms are mixed and mingled, and entire landscapes are turned into *loci amoeni* irrespective of their unpromising situations or conditions. From this perspective, Circe can be understood as more than a mythical witch of the Greco-Roman world who is revived in Renaissance literature. Rather, she might be taken as a symbolic figure or cipher for the operations of art on nature in garden and landscape design, whether this involves the union of distinct entities in new hybrid forms (of which the practice of grafting is one example) or the whole-scale imposition of an artificial scheme on the terrain.

These observations can be reduced to two main points: first, the fate of the victims of the seductive, artificial appeal of Circe and her garden serves as a warning about the dangers of submission to beauty. Second, Circe and later enchantresses personify Renaissance anxieties about the usurpation of nature by art. Both of these themes appear in the reception history of designed landscapes, from Earle's critique of Italianate fashions in Jacobean garden design, to contemporaneous concerns about the legitimacy of the practice of grafting. Most importantly, this strand of thought offers a counter-narrative to the cliché that the historical garden, especially that of the Renaissance, was universally understood as an unproblematic *locus amoenus*. In the texts that have been briefly considered here, landscape beauty is a synonym of artificiality and even depravity. Designed landscapes cannot be trusted.

Circe, then, not only provides a framework for addressing the themes of delusion, imagination, enchantment, and beauty in the early modern experience of gardens but is also symbolic of the troubling temptations that ensue from the transformations of nature by art. It might, finally, be suggested that although Circe has long since disappeared from mainstream view, the palpable anxiety about interventions in the natural world that her myths express provides an incipient historical precedent for the environmental concerns of our own period.

28 Ibid., 373.

29 Ilva Beretta, "'The World's a Garden': Garden Poetry of the English Renaissance," PhD diss., Uppsala University [1993], 95.

30 Quoted in Rebecca Bushnell, ed., *The Marvels of the World: An Anthology of Nature Writing Before 1700* [University of Pennsylvania Press, 2021], 299–300.

31 See Rebecca Bushnell, *Green Desire: Imagining Early Modern English Gardens* [Cornell University Press, 2003], 142.

32 Della Porta's third book is presented as a "marvellous compendium of every possible thing you might—or might not—want to do with fruit or flowers: to generate a plant from "putrefaction," "to make one fruit compounded of many," to have fruits and flowers "at all time[s] of the year," to grow fruit that is unusually big or without a stone, kernel, rind, or shell, to make fruits and flowers "to be of diverse colors, such as are not naturally incident to their kind" or sweeter, or to see that "fruits that are in their growing, may be made to receive and resemble all figures and impressions whatsoever." Bushnell, *Green Desire*, 142.

33 On *mescolanza* in architectural theory, see Alina Payne, "*Mescolare, Composti* and Monsters in Italian Architectural Theory of the Renaissance," in *Disarmonia, brutezza e bizzarria nel Rinascimento*, Atti del VII Convegno Internazionale, Chianciano-Pienza, July 17–20, 1995, edited by Luisa Secchi Tarugi [Franco Cesati Editore, 1998], 273–94.

34 "[M]escolando l'arte con la natura, non si sa discernere s'elle è opera di questo o di quella; anzi or altrui pare un naturale artifizio ora una artifiziosa natura." See BartolommeoTaegio, *La Villa*, trans. Thomas E. Beck [University of Pennsylvania Press, 2011], 61, for his discussion of this passage.

35 On this, see Yarnall, *Circe*, 108.

36 Ibid.

37 These are Comes's contributions to the Circe myth rather than being derived from earlier authorities.

38 Quoted in Yarnall, *Circe*, 109–10.

ASPHALT + OTHER UGLY-BEAUTIES: A MELTING LEXICON

GRETCHEN ERNSTER HENDERSON

Gretchen Ernster Henderson is a writer, artist, and a senior lecturer at the University of Texas at Austin, where she was a 2020–2022 Faculty Fellow at UT's Humanities Institute. She is the author of five books, including *Ugliness: A Cultural History* (2015) and *Life in the Tar Seeps: A Spiraling Ecology from a Dying Sea* (2023). Henderson was recently a Fellow at the Women's International Studies Center in New Mexico and Annie Clark Tanner Fellow in Environmental Humanities at the University of Utah.

➕ ENVIRONMENTAL STUDIES, ETHICS

"[T]race the course of 'absent images' in the blank spaces..."

Robert Smithson, "The Spiral Jetty"

ACCIDENT, see HEALING,
INJURY, PERCEPTION

**AESTHETICS OF SUSPICION,
see BEAUTY, UGLY**

ALGAE, see BLOOM, LAKE ERIE

ANIMAL

ASPHALT, see PAVED STREETS, TAR
SEEPS, URBAN HEAT ISLANDS

BACTERIA

BEAUTY

(BIO)DIVERSITY

BIRDS, see FLYWAYS

**BODIES (OF WATER, OF LAND),
see ANIMAL, BOTANICAL,
HUMAN, MINERAL**

BOUNDARY OBJECT, see
BODIES (OF WATER, OF LAND),
LANDSCAPE ARCHITECTURE,
QUESTIONS

Imagine a body of water as a lake, a seeming sea, saltier than oceans and vast enough to curve the horizon. This water is salty enough to crystalize, so heavy that you float and itch when you swim. Often dismissed as a dead sea in the high desert, the lake brims with life. Algae and microbes infuse its saline waters beyond blue—orange, pink, darkening to the color of blood—shifting as lake levels rise and fall. Natural asphalt oozes through tectonic fractures into sticky pools, freezing and melting around migrating birds. The lake is riddled with islands in a bathtub-like basin, with no outlet to seas, encircled by jagged mountains, and edged by humanmade composites: freeways, urban heat islands, an airport, power plants, mines, and mineral ponds, military testing zones, and suburban sprawl around public and private lands. As the human population swells, seasons cycle with diminishing snowpacks. There is less and less water. The watershed shapes the land, with tectonic shifts, as slow revelations emerge in viscous liquid. Tar seeps emerge.

Photographers "have struggled with the beauty of ugliness," writes art critic Lucy Lippard while exploring land use, politics, and art in the changing West. "Wounds on the land, sculpturally destroyed or picturesque—graphic aerial shots or colorfully polluted waters—can be so striking that the message is overwhelmed and misery or horror is merely estheticized," she writes. "On the other hand, beauty can powerfully convey difficult ideas by engaging people when they might otherwise turn away. Those who choose beauty for tragic subject matter are most effective when they're also aware of the flipside – when their choice of beauty is a conscious means to counter brutality." ***See also ENTANGLED, QUESTIONS, UGLINESS, WHAT'S NEXT?***

I came to Great Salt Lake after recovering from being hit by a car in a crosswalk—on humanmade asphalt—but it took me longer to correlate the lake's tar seeps—of natural asphalt—by comparison. Tar seeps are pools of raw oil, nicknamed "death traps," that creep up from tectonic fractures and spread across the earth like sticky flypaper. An unsuspecting bird or animal that crosses a melting seep can get fatally stuck. Great Salt Lake's tar seeps reside along its remote north shore, and over time, I witnessed a team of environmental scientists, artistic curators, land managers, and students working collaboratively to steward this challenging place. I grew to wonder why the region's namesake was often dismissed as "stinky" and "ugly": virtually hiding in plain sight. Associations of life and death, degeneration and regeneration, injury and healing, slowly started to congeal. My accident colored the backdrop against which I came to see the lake—not as dead but as wildly alive—a watershed for shifting perceptions of any overlooked place.

CHARISMATIC LANDSCAPE,
see (NON)CHARISMATIC
(-LANDSCAPE, -SPECIES)

CLASSIFICATION, (DE)
CLASSIFICATION

CLIMATE CRISIS

COLONIAL SETTLEMENT

DEAD SEA, see REPRESENTATION

In this desolate, spare landscape in the high desert—a place of surreal ugly beauty—convergences occur around adjacent jetties by the tar seeps: a straight jetty abandoned from attempts at oil drilling, and Robert Smithson's iconic earthwork of *Spiral Jetty* (1970). The massive eroding land art unfurls its coil of salt-encrusted, black basalt—15 feet wide and 1,500 feet long—three times counterclockwise into the saline lake. Created by a bulldozer, the artwork has been called aesthetically beautiful and an ugly scar. Smithson deliberately placed *Spiral Jetty* by the tar seeps to invite comparison. Some first-time visitors to Rozel Point mistake the abandoned oil jetty for Smithson's artwork.

DEATH TRAP, see TAR SEEP

"About one mile north of the oil seeps I selected my site," wrote Smithson about his chosen site for *Spiral Jetty* in 1970. "A series of seeps of heavy black oil more like asphalt occur just south of Rozel Point. For forty or more years people have tried to get oil out of this natural tar pool. Pumps coated with black stickiness rusted in the corrosive salt air. A hut mounted on pilings could have been the habitation of 'the missing link,'" he added, with "evidence of a succession of man-made systems mired in abandoned hopes." After he first visited *Spiral Jetty*, Smithson wrote, "We followed roads that glided away into dead ends. Sandy slopes turned into viscous masses of perception…an expanse of salt flats bordered the lake, and caught in its sediments were countless bits of wreckage." Shortly after he created *Spiral Jetty*, lake levels rose and covered the artwork for almost three decades.

(DE)COMPOSITION

In recent years, as Great Salt Lake has receded from drought to record low levels, the tar seeps have emerged, melting and freezing and shifting in the eye of this beholder, refocusing perceptions.

DESERT, see ALIVE, BARREN, DEAD,
(MIS/UNDER)REPRESENTATION

DIRT, see MATTER OUT OF
PLACE, UGLY, VISCOUS

Around the two jetties, the lake moves in seeming stillness. Microbial life swims, finless, in colorful saline saturation, immune to the burning sun. Microseisms emanate as faint tremors from the slowly moving planet. In winter winds can chill to the bone. Tar seeps melt through seasonal cycles. Even on a seemingly still, hot summer day, there is movement: buoyant in dense saltwater, evaporating into the atmosphere. The air can stink from bacteria, natural asphalt, and decaying matter. Vapor condenses and precipitates through cycles across mountain ranges back to the basin, through snowmelt and river runoff around the Bear River Migratory Bird Refuge, where birds flock to marshes. The Bear River Refuge sits at the convergence of two of the four major bird migratory flyways of North America and supports millions of birds.

DISAPPEAR, see DRY PLAYA

DROSSCAPE, see DISTURBED SITE,
WASTELAND, WILD/ERNESS

While *Spiral Jetty* lay underwater, microbiologists who studied the lake's colorful halophiles floated by boat over the unseen art. The earthwork remerged in 2002 with the receding lake. *Spiral Jetty* echoes a mythic whirlpool while being a bellwether of drought.

What body of water is free from landscape architecture, as all life on earth is atmospherically affected by human-driven climate change, directly or indirectly shaped, melting as glacial ice or hydrologically dammed and diverted in our thirsty world?

"Underground," a paleontologist tells me after we visit Great Salt Lake's tar seeps, "there are certain patterns where the oil gets trapped. But sometimes things happen where the oil comes to the surface, creating the tar pits. That's when you have faulting action. When you have faults or any movement, the seal gets broken…Getting the petroleum to the surface requires some type of tectonic activity—whether mountain uplift like the Wasatch front or slipping like the San Andreas fault—anything that breaks up your packets of rock so there are fractures that a fluid can percolate through. This is also how you get your geothermal springs along the front. It's very holistic – everything ties together."

How can something environmentally ugly appear aesthetically beautiful – as in injurious or injured as a colorful dying sea, algae bloom, pit mine, or *fill in the blank*? Can we cultivate care around seemingly ugly landscapes that, when revalued aesthetically, might shift human perceptions and behaviors to support biodiversity on our shared planet? In this vein, what are neglected or undervalued aesthetics of landscape architecture? **See also ENDANGERED, NEAR-EXTINCT, NON-CHARISMATIC LANDSCAPES, UGLY ANIMAL PRESERVATION SOCIETY, WORLDVIEW**

"People don't think the lake is worth anything aesthetically, biologically, or economically," an ornithologist tells me as we drive to visit the tar seeps and *Spiral Jetty*. "It's hard to study fine-grain questions because it's hard for scientists to get out there. But we want people to steward the lake. It's a place of paradoxes. It doesn't have an icon. Who connects to brine shrimp and microbes? People come expecting to find romantic red rock but don't find it. It's stinky. You go out and find dead birds. You float and itch when you swim. There are all these funny, weird things about Great Salt Lake that aren't always described."

Whenever I fly into the Great Salt Lake basin, my face presses to the plane window for a bird's-eye view. Unlike the black tar seeps, the lake's salt evaporation ponds rivet through colors—turquoise, sea green, olive, sienna—in geometric fields like abstract paintings against the granite Wasatch Mountains. The scale is disorienting, as if those mineral ponds might lie under a microscope, floating in a Petri dish. The aesthetic is economic, signaling industries generated from the lake: salt evaporation for water softeners and de-icing; brine shrimp cyst harvesting for fish food; potassium sulfate for crop fertilizer; magnesium for auto parts, soda cans, cell phones, and pharmaceuticals. From the air, in the distance you can see Salt Lake City glint, except when the city is seasonally shrouded by inversions of trapped pollution. The scarred slope of Rio Tinto Kennecott gapes as an open pit copper mine, where a massive landslide caused human-triggered earthquakes. Carbon emissions grow with industries and infrastructure, as the population swells and uses more water. As agricultural runoff, toxic dumps, pollution, and other threats impede the lake's life, birds that feed here can die or migrate and take toxins elsewhere.

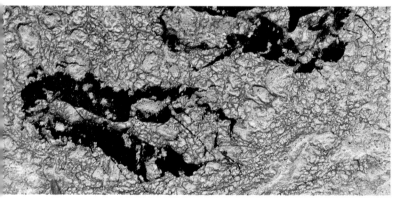 

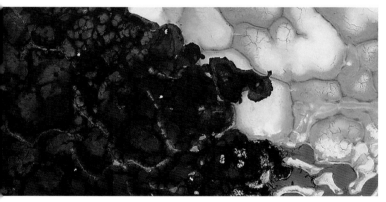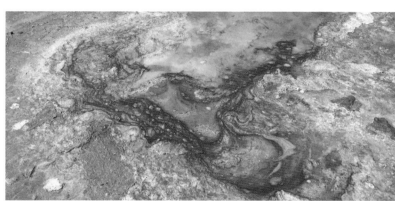

HEALING

The ornithologist calls *what is unseen* the lake's underbelly, also referring to it as *the lake's memory*. I wonder how Great Salt Lake remembers: as a body of water. When a masseuse kneads an ache in my thigh where the SUV hit me, she says, "*The body remembers*." If the body keeps the score, this does not seem limited to human bodies, also related to bodies of water and of land. In Arches National Park, several hours southeast of here, signs tell visitors not to cross certain rocks due to risks of damaging Indigenous rock art: HEALING IN PROGRESS: PLEASE STAY ON DESIGNATED TRAILS ONLY. Perhaps the lake's memories accumulate to impact its existence over time, flooding and receding, the way personal events compress. Even as events fade in our minds, our bodies remember: with an ache or stiffness, sensitivity to noise, a residual imprint. Tectonics suggest that stones remember in their way, storing up tensions until they quake. The lake may remember through erosion, dispersion, or seepage.

HEARTBEAT, see BODIES (OF WATER, OF LAND)

"This is the heartbeat," says the ornithologist of Great Salt Lake and the rivers that feed its water cycle in a basin with no outlets to the sea. It is a land of interdependent entrapment. "It's the place of transformation. The arteries that go into the lake look like what's going into your body."

HERE

A walk on the rocky foothold of *Spiral Jetty* unfocuses its coil, inviting a visitor to cycle through the expansive landscape: from mudflats and tar seeps across the lake, to islands and mountains, clouds and sky. The otherworldly landscape swallows a body into the reality of its smallness, the gravity of its orbit. Seemingly isolated, relationships heighten. Actions recalibrate. Each movement demands presence. Senses awaken beyond sight. Life reduces elementally. Human presence is thrown into relief as perceptions (de)form around how we (de)value any place. To walk the mudflats, surrounded by natural death traps in a reputedly dead sea, blurs life across time and place. Separations melt: I to we. Under our skins thrive microbial ecosystems. Sloshing in our ears, biorhythms reverberate as microseisms, humming as a heartbeat, or the ancient music of the spheres. In a seemingly timeless yet timestamped landscape, dormancy turns agency. Urgency. Everything is here, there, then, and now. In danger of getting stuck in habitual traps, a footprint evokes a human body; a feather conjures a bird.

HOME, see BODY, EARTH, ECOLOGY

HOPE, see *FILL IN THE BLANK*

Feel your body wherever you are, placing: your muscle tensions, posture, heat or cool. Listen. Breathe under your skin. Smell the air. Notice how your body connects with the ground. Feel the earth beneath your feet. Nudge your toes and fingers. Sense how any movement, each breath, enlivens other parts of your body and the space around you. Breathe. Imagine sensory connections with other bodies, not only human and animal, but also bodies of land and bodies of water, elemental as air, sunlight, and soil. How might other bodies around you feel?

INJURY, see AGENCY, DIS/ABILITY, HUMAN, KNOWLEDGES

INSCRIPTION

Both *Spiral Jetty* and the tar seeps have disappeared and reemerged over decades with the rising and retreating great lake. They appear side-by-side both as earthworks—one made by humans, the other nature-made—and articulations beyond words. They also provoke questions around many kinds of marks that we make on this earth. Naturally etched shorelines mark ancient lake levels, crisscrossed by tectonic faults, beside natural tar seeps, so-called "death traps" that smudge the edge of a reputedly dead sea. In a fairly wild landscape, human marks appear as abandoned attempts at oil drilling, near a dirt road through fenced ranchlands, in a state known for indigenous rock art. As different meanings seep to the surface, interconnections stick together: here and elsewhere, then and now, you and me.

KIN, KINSHIP

"In indigenous ways of knowing," writes Robin Wall Kimmerer, "other species are recognized not only as persons, but also as teachers who can inspire how we might live. We can learn a new solar economy from plants, medicines from mycelia, and architecture from the ants."

KNOWLEDGES, see BODIES (OF WATER, OF LAND)

LAND ACKNOWLEDGMENT

Understanding that Indigenous land acknowledgments are inadequate if they are words without actions, I acknowledge that this land currently called Utah, named for the Ute tribe, is the unceded, traditional, and ancestral homeland of the Shoshone, Paiute, Goshute, and Ute tribes, whose members have been and continue to be stewards of the land currently called Utah.

LAND ART, see (DE)COMPOSITION, ENTROPY, EROSION, LAND ARTS OF THE AMERICAN WEST, POSTCOMMODITY, WHAT NEXT?

Against the lake, *Spiral Jetty* is relatively small. Photographs exaggerate its size and scale, centering what otherwise decentralizes. In aerial photography, *Spiral Jetty* becomes the focal point. As with other land art, photographs cannot replace the work. Attempts to represent or border it reveal the limitations of the work and any medium, expose the view of a creator, lose what lies at the edge or outside the frame. To some degree land art's resistance to being reproduced (even literally through copyright restrictions, including our own photographs) forces attention beyond the object to the place it occupies, what (and who) lies adjacent and overlooked, as questions arise about what gets attention and what is undervalued.

LAND ETHIC

LANDSCAPE ARCHITECTURE, see also ARCHAEOLOGY, CENTER FOR ART+ENVIRONMENT, CENTER FOR LAND USE INTERPRETATION, DECENTERING, *FILL IN THE BLANK*

LIQUID, LIQUIFYING, see LEAKING

LISTEN
LOVE, see CARE, NEGLECT, RESPECT

MATTER OUT OF PLACE, see DIRT, NOT, UGLY

As natural asphalt bubbles up from underground sludge and creeps across the face of the earth, the landscape around Great Salt Lake resists easy classifications and interpretations: of what is valued and not, of beauty and ugliness, of purity and ruin, of benefit and loss, of access and distance, of place and displacement. Binaries break down. Fear and hope. Danger and safety. Conserved and wasted. Wounded and healed. In a world characterized by oppositions, Rozel Point reveals the wide gray space between.

MELT

Verb (abridged). **1**: *to reduce from a solid to a liquid state usually by heat · **2**: to cause to disappear or disperse · **3**: to make tender or gentle, soften. As in, to make or become liquified by heat; or, to make or become more tender or loving.*

METAPHOR, see NOT A METAPHOR

MIGRATORY

As a living body of water, Great Salt Lake sits at the convergence of two of the four major migratory bird flyways, as more human lives migrate to its shores and depend on its waters. At a glance it may be easy to dismiss the lake as lifeless or dead, stinky or ugly, until we listen: to its birds and other inhabitants, to absences amid presences of cultural histories, to those who care for its tar and art, salt and water, watering or depleting many forms of the lake's life. What is (not) here (between the lines) calls for response. Our individual actions press into lives beyond our own—not only human and animal bodies, but also bodies of land and bodies of water—resonating in ways that, if listened to, might helpfully decenter our individual selves from the center of any story.

MINE, see MINING

MILITARY TESTING, see DOWNWINDERS, NEVADA TEST SITE

NARRATIVES, see APOCALYPTIC, ELEGIAC, PASTORAL, SPECULATIVE, etc.

Like a massive ink blot on the planet, the tar seep seems to defy language, even as we grope to articulate its qualities: from fossilizing terms of paleontology, to feathered vocabulary of ornithology, to economic values of extracted oil. Without understanding the timescale of tar, I analogize it through associations and even memories. Even as I acquire terms, the seep evades classification. As tar sticks things together, it challenges a human tendency to classify: disarticulating anything that gets trapped.

NATURAL AGENCY

Ultimately, the tar seep will swallow all languages that attempt to describe it. Bacteria break it down. Destruction and creation all rolled into one. As some bacteria even eat tar, they suggest hope for cleaning up future oil spills, and something more philosophical: about the power of microbial species, integral to our life cycles. Bacteria line our guts, maintain our body chemistry, and one day decompose us back to dirt—unless we get stuck in a tar seep. Tar seeps offer a reminder to watch where we step, to question human acts and scales in relation to the agency of the Earth.

NON-SITES, see SITES

NOT A METAPHOR, see CLIMATE CRISIS, DECOLONIZATION

NOT SEEING, see PERCEPTION, REPRESENTATION

OIL, see FOSSIL FUEL, OIL SPILL, TAR SANDS

OXYGEN, see RIVERS, WATER

The water level of Great Salt Lake is at a historically recorded low.

OUTSIDE THE FRAME, see ELSEWHERE, HERE

PELICANS, see BIRDS, FLYWAYS, GREAT SALT LAKE

Riveted by tar seeps, I barely think of humanmade asphalt, of the car hitting me, of my head bouncing off the metal hood and meshing with pavement. I try to imagine how pelicans land in tar seeps; I don't think of my scalp stapled back together, of a walker supporting my steps, of rearticulating language over months, relearning to physically move, read, and write. The tar seeps wouldn't be mistaken for streets, but animals who cross this hot asphalt get stuck and die. Slower than a car crash, the seeps enact a different kind of collision – yet with both, you don't realize you're stuck until it's too late.

PETRO-AESTHETICS

Before *Spiral Jetty*, Smithson worked with asphalt and proposed artworks including *Tar Pool and Gravel Pit, Asphalt Spiral, Series of Eleven Asphalt Pavements*, and *Asphalt on Eroded Cliff*. A quarry near Rome, Italy, become the site of his sizable melt, *Asphalt Rundown* (1969). In an essay on "A Sedimentation of the Mind," he wrote of his attraction to "tar" that "makes one conscious of the primal ooze…a tertiary world of petroleum, asphalts, ozocerite, and bituminous agglomerations."

PLACE, see (DIS/MIS)PLACE, MATTER OUT OF PLACE, MIGRATORY

Drawing on anthropologist Mary Douglass's theory of *dirt* as "matter out of place," architectural theorist Mark Cousins writes, "all speculation about ugliness travels through the realm of what it is not." What *is not* landscape architecture also *is*. As perceptions shift, so do relations between objects-being-perceived and subjects-who-are-perceiving, with the capacity to shift interrelations between:

POETICS OF SPACE

QUESTIONS, see *FILL IN THE BLANKS*

"The purpose of art," writes James Baldwin, "is to lay bare the questions that have been hidden by the answers."

RECIPROCITY

RELATIONAL

REPRESENTATION, see ART, SALT, LAKE, OIL, SENSORY, TAR, WATER

RUNDOWN

SCALE

SIGHT, see VIEWER, LISTENING, SMELLING, TOUCHING

SEEPAGE

"People know pelicans," the ornithologist tells me. "They have those enormous bills. They're beautiful and charismatic. They're one of the signature birds of the area and may be a way for people to care about the lake. If we could connect people to pelicans, we could connect them to uphill water diversions, climate change, and impacted marshlands."

A recurring motif through human-driven environmental disasters, particularly oil spills, is a pelican coated in tar. Pelicans are a charismatic species, like polar bears are poster animals for melting polar icecaps. Birds coated in tar are not newly associated with the environmental distress. In 1969, a year before the creation of Spiral Jetty, a massive oil spill off the coast of Santa Barbara, California (near the Carpinteria Oil Seeps and Tar Pits) featured tar-coated birds. Other oil spills—from the Exxon Valdez in Prince William Sound of Alaska in 1989 to Deepwater Horizon in the Gulf of Mexico in 2010—similarly show tarred birds on the verge of dying or already dead. Have these images done anything to change human behavior as the climate crisis hits a tipping point?

To feel *rundown*, as in: depleted, declining, exhausted. *Rundown*, as a noun: declining as Robert Smithson's sizable melting *Asphalt Rundown* (1969). A rundown can be a summary, like an abstract of an essay (like this) compressing into fossilized form, where only bits remain: *This essay gathers terminology around neglected aesthetics in landscapes to decenter associations of ugliness and beauty in landscape design. The alphabetized entries enact a verbal stratigraphy through micro-essays around a particular landscape—Great Salt Lake with its tar seeps of natural asphalt—to erode separations between ugly/beauty, urban/wild, life/death, human/nonhuman, dead/living, built/natural, to suggest the wide gray space between binaries where interrelations may grow. As the lake's tar seeps provoke non-familiarized, multisensory, embodied ways of perceiving, they exert nonhuman agency around extracted sites of natural resources, heightening attentions to neglected aesthetics and overlooked ecologies. What is next? The essay's formal categorization exposes its limitations, in essence decategorizing or melting into a productive failure, running down…*

Scale can be measured cartographically or chronologically (as timescales), both graduated to indicate a relationship between distances. A scale also measures weight. Or scaling, as in climbing—to scale a mountain—or a skin-like sheath, as scales encrust a fish or delicately coat a moth's wing. There is a musical scale: a sequential series of musical tones, descending or ascending. Amid increasing dissonances across the world, what scaled possibilities might we be overlooking or, to say another way, underhearing?

Seeing is forgetting the name of the thing one sees, goes a saying not necessarily dependent on physiological sight. Sensory engagements can shift ways of seeing and being: shifting perceptions and (in)actions by reimaging our places in the world.

Asphalt's melting aesthetics of ugly beauty lend themselves to thinking about human and nonhuman agents in built environments, as the natural landscape asserts agency by intervening and collaborating in landscape design (more apparent in an urban environment like Los Angeles, built around the La Brea Tar Pits, than at Great Salt Lake's remote north shore). Yet all interconnect. The lake's story continues seeping around tectonic plates that quake and fracture, so raw oil creeps to the earth's surface as tar seeps: quiet reminders that we are all stuck together.

8/11/2018 5:06PM   8/11/2018 5:06PM   8/11/2018 5:07PM

SPIRAL, see (BIO)DIVERSITY

The spiral is a shape of expansion: from *Spiral Jetty*, to chiseled spirals in rock art, to swirling water down a drain. The shape is as seen as unseen: infinitesimal as a microbial crystal or DNA helix, or cosmic as the galaxy of the Milky Way.

SLOW STREETS, see ASPHALT DIET, FOSSIL FUEL

SLOW VIOLENCE

SNOWPACK, see DESERTIFICATION, DRY PLAYAS, GLOBAL WARMING, RISING SEA LEVELS

As drought and desertification increase across the planet, might "dead" and "ugly" landscapes widen perceptive registers of environmental beauty, teaching humans to live, survive, and even thrive through fewer resources, doing more with less, suggesting more sustainable possibilities for other species and ecosystems across the planet?

SOLAR SYSTEM

At Great Salt Lake, Smithson described his artwork as a "time machine," where "The scale of the *Spiral Jetty* tends to fluctuate depending on where the viewer happens to be…A crack in the wall if viewed in terms of scale, not size, could be called the Grand Canyon. A room could be made to take on the immensity of the solar system."

STRATIGRAPHY

STICKY, STUCK

TAR SANDS

TAR SEEPS, see FOSSIL, FUTURE, NATURAL ASPHALT, OIL, PAST, PETROLEUM, PRESENT

TIME

UGLY, see AESTHETICS OF SUSPICION, BEAUTIFUL, DECOMPOSING, MELTING, RUIN, SUBLIME, VISCOUS, WASTELAND, etc. etc. etc.

There's much more to say – about aesthetics of climate change, about multisensory perception, about non-charismatic landscapes and species, environmental injury and healing, as architectural developments can (de)value relations between humans and landscapes. Ugliness etymologically derives from what is feared or dreaded, with cultural consequences, influencing how humans turn away from not only people but also places. Many overlooked sites await the art of attention. As landscapes dismissed as "ugly" interrelate with biodiversity, species like microbes (interrelated with the human gut) have garnered attention along with "imperfect" and "misfit" and "fallen" fruit and vegetables to discourage food waste, decomposing (composting) natural resources to regenerate ecosystems, and…and…and. Landscape architecture offers impermanent thresholds, portals, borders, and organic materials that overgrow and grow into the agency of the evolving earth.

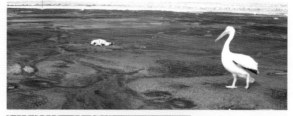

8/11/2018   5:07PM

8/18/2018   10:27AM

UNDERGROUND, see AQUIFER, FAULTLINE, OIL, TECTONIC, WATER

UNDERHEARING, see HEARTBEAT, NERVOUS SYSTEM, NOT SILENT, RESILIENCE, RESONANCE

VIEWER, see BEYOND SIGHT, MULTISENSORY, NOT SEEING, VIEWSHED, WAYS OF SEEING

VISCOUS, see STICKY

WATER, see LIQUID, LIFE, WATER RIGHTS, WATER SECURITY, WATERSHED

WHAT'S NEXT?   . . .

Are liquid landscapes ever isolated? Evaporation, condensation, precipitation, runoff, infiltration, uptake, transpiration, continuing the water cycle under our shared planetary atmosphere. As this living planet tilts the axis of our knowledges, what is ugly and beautiful function like binary stars, falling into each other's gravity and orbiting each other in an expanding universe, while constellating with many other shifting stars.

Quoted sources (in order of appearance): Jack Flam (ed.), *Robert Smithson: The Collected Writings* (University of California Press, 1996) • Lucy R. Lippard, *Undermining: A Wild Ride through Land Use, Politics, and Art in the Changing West* (The New Press, 2014) • Personal interviews with "paleontologist" and "ornithologist" include H. Greg McDonald, Western regional paleontologist for the Bureau of Land Management, and Jaimi Butler, coordinator of the Great Salt Lake Institute, conducted in Utah in 2018–2019; see Gretchen E. Henderson, "Life in the Tar Seeps," *Ecotone* 28 (2019) and gretchenhenderson.com/life-in-the-tar-seeps • Robin Wall Kimmerer, "Nature Needs a New Pronoun: To Stop the Age of Extinction, Let's Start by Ditching 'It,'" *Yes! Magazine* (2015) • Mark Cousins, "The Ugly," in Dave Beech (ed.), *Beauty: Documents of Contemporary Art* (MIT Press, 2009) • James Baldwin quoted in Claudia Rankine, *Citizen: An American Lyric* (Graywolf, 2014) • **Terms by scholars include** "aesthetics of suspicion" (Kathleen Marie Higgins) • "boundary object" (Susan Leigh Star and James R. Griesemer) • "charismatic landscapes" (Betsey A. Robinson and Elise Hunchuck) • "decolonization is not a metaphor" (Eve Tuck and K. Wayne Yang) • "desegregating wilderness (Jourdan Imani Keith) • "Indigenous futurisms" (Grace Dillon) • "Land Arts of the American West" (Chris Taylor), alongside scholars, artists, and curators affiliated with the Center for Art + Environment at the Nevada Museum of Art, Center for Land Use Interpretation, Dia Art Foundation, Holt/Smithson Foundation, Postcommodity, Utah Museum of Fine Arts, and related organizations and collectives • "land ethic" (Aldo Leopold) • "matter out of place" (Mary Douglass) • "petro-aesthetics" (Stephanie LeMenager) • "poetics of space" (Gaston Bachelard) • "slow violence" (Rob Nixon) • Excerpts of the author's projects on *Ugliness: A Cultural History* (Reaktion, 2015) and *Life in the Tar Seeps: A Spiraling Ecology from a Dying Se*a (Trinity University Press, 2023) seep between the lines.

Acknowledgment: Grateful acknowledgment is made to the Great Salt Lake Institute (GSLI) at Westminster College for permission to reproduce their camera trap images. The GSLI continually works to steward Great Salt Lake with collaborative partners.

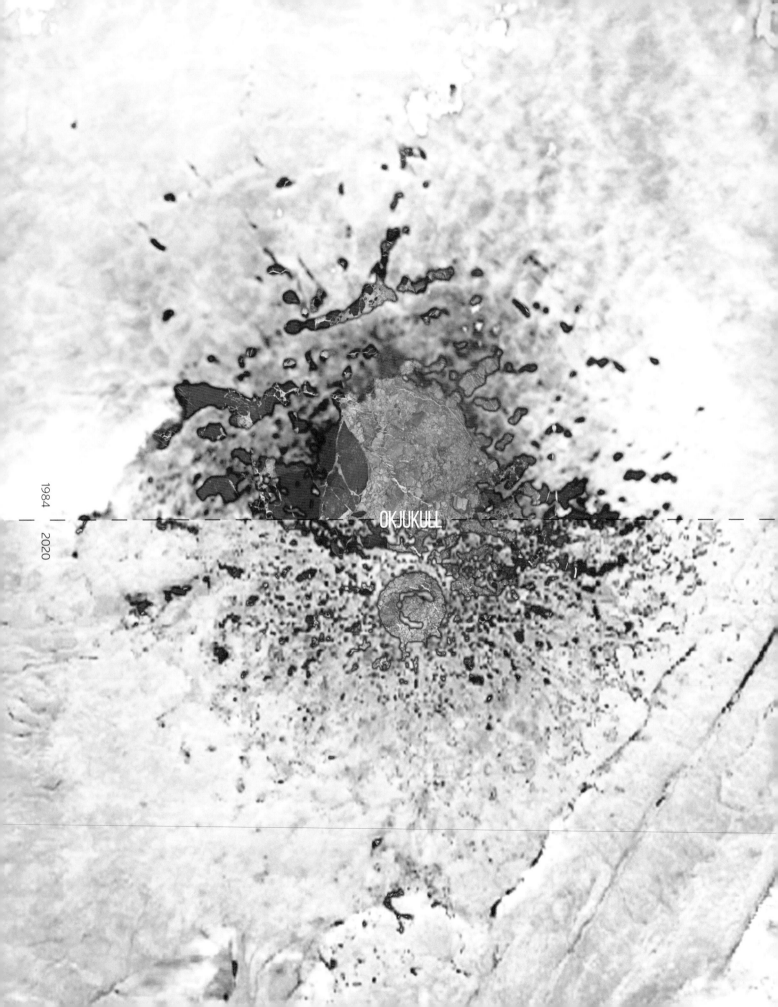

1984

2020

OKJUKULL

DAN VAN DER HORST + SASKIA VERMEYLEN
BEAUTIFUL EYESORES
WAYS OF SEEING WIND ENERGY

Dan van der Horst is Professor of Energy, Environment & Society at the University of Edinburgh. He studies societal transitions towards environmental sustainability, seeking to understand why progress on the ground has been so geographically uneven, mostly slow and often unfair. Dan has written extensively on the emergence of new energy landscapes, paying special attention to how citizens (can) engage with cleaner energy technologies.

Saskia Vermeylen is a Reader in Law at the University of Strathclyde, Glasgow. She is a socio-legal property scholar, and her research focuses on critiquing liberal property theories from multiple perspectives drawing upon continental philosophy, phenomenology, posthumanism, and cultural studies. She is also a curator and has recently completed a Leverhulme fellowship on space law, utopian literatures and art.

+ ENERGY POLICY, AESTHETICS

The funeral was held at the site where Ok died. It was a bleak landscape on the flat top of a dormant volcano, the ceremony was attended by artists, activists, and government ministers. A copper plate on a stone was revealed, saying *"This monument is to acknowledge that we know what is happening and what needs to be done."* What is happening is climate change. Ok's full name was Okjukull, a 700-year-old glacier that was pronounced dead in 2014. Iceland still has 269 named glaciers, but all are expected to disappear in the next 200 years, unless we do what needs to be done: drastically reduce greenhouse gas emissions into the atmosphere. Icelanders seem to care about their glaciers, and they can see their landscapes change dramatically due to anthropogenic climate change. The thinly populated country already has big hydropower and geothermal plants, enabling them to produce all their electricity and heat without the need for fossil fuel. Iceland's abundance of cheap carbon-neutral electricity has attracted electricity hungry industries like aluminum smelters and data centers. But the expansion of renewables is contested, with some Icelanders fearing that it would spoil outdoor experiences because the "visual effects are so strong."[1] In particular, the idea of wind farm development is perceived as making the stark landscape in the Icelandic highlands less beautiful.

The unpopulated highlands of Iceland could not be more different from densely populated England, but here, too, concerns about "unsightly" wind farms have been raised time and again. Despite overwhelming public support for climate change action and for wind power in general, as well as bipartisan political support for decarbonizing the UK, in 2015 the Conservative government decided to allow local councils in England to block onshore wind farm development, thus effectively putting a stop to the cheapest type of renewable energy generation. The current energy crisis and unprecedented costs of oil and gas sparked by Vladimir Putin's invasion of the Ukraine have dramatically changed the logic for wind energy development.

In the past, this technology received financial support through national climate change mitigation policies. Onshore wind has become cheaper than fossil fuel-based electricity generation and now it is suddenly also recognized for its contribution to national energy security. But in late 2022 the new UK Prime Minister Rishi Sunak was considering reversing this policy, and many Conservative members of parliament representing rural English constituencies continue to resist onshore wind on the ground of aesthetic concerns.

So here we have two very different countries (culturally, politically, economically) with entirely different types of landscapes, and yet we find the very same concern raised about the aesthetics of landscapes with turbines. Many academics have studied public perceptions of renewables and have been satisfied to simply report that people hold a wide range of views about the "landscape" impacts of wind farms, ranging from positive to negative. There have been efforts to explain opposition to wind farms in terms of place identity, perceived risks, lack of local benefits, lack of consultation, and mistrust in institutions. However, very few have recognized the need, let alone tried, to unpack this aesthetic assertion by opponents to wind farms. We try to remedy this. By examining both wind turbines and the everyday landscapes in which they are sited, we aim to bring theories of beauty and aesthetic appreciation into the conversation about public perceptions of wind farm development.

Wind turbines are machines to mine wind energy and their highly standardized design is strictly functional. To consider them through the lens of aesthetics would thus logically require a consideration of what they do. This is the realm of *functional beauty*, a topic explored by Glenn Parsons and Allen Carlson in their book of the same name.[2] It is also important to recognize that our aesthetic appreciation of wind farms is different from the more conventional foci of aesthetic appreciation. Neither turbines nor most landscapes are sublime examples of beauty or indeed seen as "art" in the more narrow or traditional sense, which we tend to encounter in unique locations (such as museums and national parks) and/or through special frames (such as pictures on a wall, statues on a pedestal, plays in a theater, or music through headphones). We may encounter proposed wind farms in the media that we consume in everyday life, and we may see real windfarms in our daily environment, or as we travel for reasons entirely unrelated to wind farms. In other words, we are dealing here with *everyday aesthetics* – the title of Yuriko Saito's book.[3] Deploying these two texts, we seek to understand how wind turbines in everyday landscapes might be considered "beautiful," and what—from the perspective of aesthetic theories of functional beauty—may render them "ugly." Let us start with a disclaimer, by positing (1) that functional beauty is important but not necessarily exclusive for aesthetic appreciation (what Parsons and Carlson call a "weak" take on functional beauty); and (2) that the ecological value of an object does not automatically determine its aesthetic value (what Saito calls "environmental determinism").

To elucidate the notion of functional beauty, Parsons and Carlson frame a dialogue between the philosophical positions on beauty taken by Socrates and David Hume. For Socrates, beauty is being well adapted to a purpose, while for Hume, beauty is not just fitness to any purpose – it must have utility for humankind. Socrates's view draws attention to the role of knowledge with regard to function and how this knowledge can be obtained: for a thing to be deemed beautiful, Socrates thinks that it suffices to observe that the thing *seems* fit for purpose. It could be argued that this mobilizes two separate forms of knowledge: the mainly visual characteristics of things that make them appear to be fit for purpose and a deeper knowledge about the likely effectiveness of the thing to perform its function in practice. This potentially opens the door for a comparative debate: for example, about the functional beauty of different wind turbine designs where more or bigger blades may look better suited to catch wind, but the thinner three-blade design has proven more efficient in practice.

Hume's narrower definition of functional beauty raises questions of morality (should we attribute utility to a tool designed for hurting people?) and positionality (for whom is the tool useful?), which he seeks to address by invoking an additional aspect: sympathy with others. Thus, a thing is beautiful if it can be observed to have utility for someone else, even if it has none for the observer.

A wind turbine's ability to generate electricity, evidenced by the visual observation of rotating blades, constitutes a fitness to function and explicit utility. A working wind turbine is thus clearly a thing of functional beauty. Conversely, a wind turbine that is not turning, is more difficult to assess. If we have information to suggest that it has just stopped turning because the wind speed has dropped below the minimum threshold, then we could say that the functional beauty of the turbine has been temporarily suspended, but we cannot say that the turbine has become dysfunctional. However, if turbines are observed to be immobile for long periods of time due to the wind being too weak or too strong, this opens a potential avenue to question the fitness of the location or the technology, which in turn may lead to a less favorable assessment in terms of functional beauty. Within a windfarm, we might observe that some turbines are turning and one is not. We could then surmise that this particular turbine is broken or badly placed. It is therefore no longer fit for its purpose – its evident dysfunctionality renders it ugly.

The assessment of functional beauty seems to befit comparative approaches, not only between neighboring wind turbines in a wind farm or between different wind turbine designs and different wind farm locations, but also between different sizes of wind turbines. Because of the quadratic relationship between wind turbine height and the wind catchment area of the blades, plus the fact that the wind blows harder when you get further from the ground, bigger wind turbines are inherently more efficient in capturing wind energy. A positive scale factor in functional beauty may seem to be counterintuitive when opponents to wind farms often cite the size of the turbines as being a problem, and when aesthetic design criteria seem to stress the need to reduce the visual intrusion and spatial footprint of a wind farm. One potential way to address this problem of scale is to take a demand-side view: how much energy do we actually need within a chosen geographical area? This also allows us to consider the options to reduce demand and thus limit the need for windfarm developments in the first place.

Democratizing the debate on how much energy we really need and how we can produce (much of) it locally, may allow us to refine the discussion on functional beauty because it specifies the beneficiaries of wind energy generation. Some critiques of wind farms have focused on the characteristics of the electricity system they feed into. As an example of potentially critical technical characteristics, some grids have enough hydropower to provide back-up generation whereas others still depend on fossil-fuel plants for back-up. In addition, some environmentally harmful industrial electricity users or energy wasting industries like Bitcoin mining may be criticized for drawing upon wind energy.

Critical socio-economic grid characteristics include the costing structure for consumers (e.g., the lack of social tariffs for people in energy poverty) and, especially in the Global South, the question of energy access: do renewable energy projects actually provide poor local communities with more access to electricity that is affordable, safe, and reliable? However, it is important to recognize that it is very rarely the case that wind-power is directly responsible for such environmental and social problems. We would argue that (knowledge of) these grid characteristics should affect mainly how we view the existing grid system and its governance. The criticism is misdirected if we question the functional beauty of a new wind farm that does not provide electricity access to the local community, when it is the exclusionary local grid connection that is ugly and needs fixing.

This example illustrates that functional beauty in a more complex socio-material context like a landscape is much more difficult to define. Parsons and Carlson engage with questions of dysfunction and indeterminacy of function across a range of things, from art and artifacts to buildings and nature. In the case of human-made objects, they posit that function is observed through historic development and market forces; while in the case of living nature, it is observed through the lens of natural selection. This epistemological position makes it harder to apply the concept of functional beauty to novel artifacts but also to a landscape, which is largely made of non-living, inorganic things. The environmental philosopher Holmes Rolston, known for his work on the intrinsic values of living nature, is quoted as saying "the scenery cannot fail, because nothing is attempted." As a contextual nuance to this statement, the position of the human observer matters to the scenic quality that is revealed. Perceiving the scenery could potentially "fail," for example, if nearby trees have grown so high that they block the scenic view or if the viewing location is crowded, noisy, or full of litter.

Parsons and Carlson briefly acknowledge that ecologists recognize ecosystem functions and see this as one possible way in which a landscape could still succeed and thus be deemed beautiful. However, it is surprising that they do not recognize that this also makes the opposite possible. For example, the disappearance of glaciers can damage riparian habitats and freshwater ecosystems. Thus, global warming creates a new or changed landscape that is no longer fit to continue its pre-existing ecosystem functions. The landscape could thus be said to have lost functional beauty. Successful climate change mitigation requires a huge growth in renewable energy – wind energy included. Wind farms can thus be said to help protect landscape functions and therefore also help maintain the functional beauty of the landscape. Where there is an attempt to capture and utilize the wind, the landscape can be said to have gained in functionality. But for some landscape users, the local landscape may also lose in functionality because of the disruption of a sense of tranquility that hinges on the visual absence of permanent markers of modern society.

Furthermore, the contribution of a single wind farm to climate change mitigation is small, indirect, and diffuse over space and time and it does not negate the risk of more direct negative impacts on nonhumans, for example if a windfarm is built in a fragile natural habitat or along the migration route of endangered bat or bird species that might die at the blades of a wind turbine. These examples may serve as a critique against the rather anthropocentric roots of functional beauty.

How can we reconcile Rolston's idea that "the scenery cannot fail," with the strong empirical evidence that humans tend to find some landscapes more beautiful than others? We propose that this tension can be resolved with a proviso that Rolston's statement is categorical about landscape, rather than comparative between landscapes. Moreover, our focus in this essay is on normal and widespread landscapes rather than on famous and iconic landscapes, which are often visually familiar to us through paintings, photographs, and film. These iconic landscapes, picturesque and often legally protected, are already "framed" and imbued with an expectation of permanence that, as Saito observes, is a western metaphysical priority and a characteristic expectation in western paradigmatic art. She argues that the frameless nature of non-art objects, including ordinary or everyday landscapes, can be "compensated by exercising our imagination and creativity in constituting the aesthetic object as we see fit." Indeed, she suggests that the unfamiliar can invite and stimulate our thinking about and engagement with the aesthetics of everyday things. By that logic, it could be argued that the insertion of a foreign object into the landscape, like a wind turbine, could in fact help to catalyze and stimulate the development of a stronger aesthetic awareness. Saito speaks in relatively generic terms about the importance of ecological literacy in shaping aesthetic appreciation, but others have noted the presence of a more place-based aesthetics where local residents show a positive appreciation of material things in the landscape that non-locals would consider less positively. Finally, we can observe an inherent contradiction in opponents' landscape concerns, which tend to be the strongest during the period that a new windfarm is proposed. Expressed through visual metaphors like "eyesores," opponents are referring to objects that do not yet exist and thus cannot be seen or otherwise encountered in the material world. They must be imagined and framed and indeed they often are, visually, through artists' impressions, photomontage, or cartoons.

With respect to landscape, Saito's everyday aesthetics shares some important similarities with the more-than-representational turn in cultural geography, which (moving away from the pictorial) draws more attention to doing, performing, affect, and practice. Saito's thinking on how the everyday aesthetics of landscape is experienced, would appear to align particularly well with anthropologist Tim Ingold's concept of dwelling in the landscape, which embraces multi-sensory encounters to challenge the hegemony of the visual and which counters the expectation of landscape permanence by embracing temporal perspectives. This rich, embodied, and situated encounter with and in the landscape is not possible with proposed wind farms, but it is much more common with existing wind farms, and it is therefore no surprise that existing wind farms yield far fewer negative aesthetic responses. While everyday aesthetics is not particularly suited to yield clear and unequivocal judgement on the beauty of a landscape with wind turbines, it can certainly help to dismiss categorical truth claims about ugliness. However, it does so by demanding that we have regular, inclusive, and full access to the landscape; that we are allowed to dwell there. In practice this implies that the access roads created to build wind farms on private land should generally serve to increase public access, and wind farms on public land should not be fenced off.

The eye cannot see a proposed wind farm. Nor can it see the greenhouse gases we are currently dumping into the atmosphere or the diffuse and complex climate change effects these are causing. It is the latter (climate change) that the performers of Ok's state funeral tried to make visible, and the former (our emissions) that they spell out on that copper plate. And given these multiple invisibilities, it is important to try to tease out far more precisely what some opponents of wind farms consider to be "unsightly" or "eyesores"; how and when that judgement is reached, and why. Similarly, it is important to lay bare the arguments and interrogate the cognitive processes resulting in conclusions about the lack of fitness of the technology or damage to society through its deployment. A better understanding of these arguments and cognitive processes will enable us to expose and refute negative responses that are rooted in short-term thinking or selfish priorities, or gaps in literacy about anthropogenic climate change and the urgent need to transition our energy systems away from fossil fuels. Similarly, it will enable us to better recognize and internalize fair criticism and improve the ways in which and the places where we seek to capture wind energy – which is, of course, only one of a number of complementary mitigation and adaptation activities that we need to deploy in order to address the climate emergency. Indeed, it might well be possible to draw on these very same two theories to reach negative conclusions about the aesthetic merits of a particular wind turbine or specific wind farm location, but this too would require a far greater precision of language and argument. In other words, we cannot allow the development of a new windfarm to be blocked because some protesters make the claim that it is an eyesore. But if we want to learn more about beauty and how others may view it, then we still need to hear out anyone who starts their argument with, "It is an eyesore *because*..."

1 See works by Icelandic academic Anna Sæþórsdóttir.

2 Glenn Parsons & Allen Carlson, *Functional Beauty* (Oxford University Press, 2008).

3 Yuriko Saito, *Everyday Aesthetics* (Oxford University Press, 2007).

LAKE SIHL
INVENTING A HYDROELECTRIC LANDSCAPE

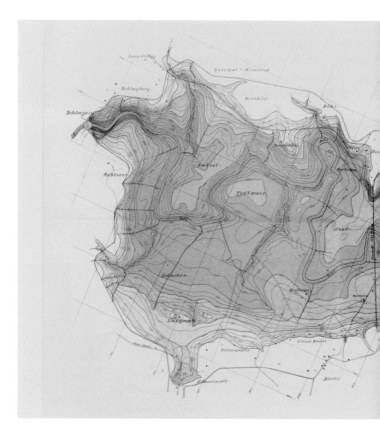

SAREM SUNDERLAND

Sarem Sunderland is a landscape architect and researcher based in Zurich, Switzerland, and Munich, Germany. He is currently writing a doctoral thesis on the relationship between hydroelectric infrastructures and landscape at ETH Zurich. Sunderland is a founding member of the architecture collective la-clique and a board member of the Swiss Federation of Landscape Architects for the regional group of Zurich.

✛ LANDSCAPE ARCHITECTURE, HISTORY

Dams are omnipresent on waterways in Switzerland to the point that they've become a key element of national identity. Yet, despite the interest that landscape architecture has built in infrastructure over the past few decades—particularly in terms of transportation and flood protection—infrastructures of hydropower remain outside the scope of the discipline. With a few notable exceptions, such as the works of the Tennessee Valley Authority (TVA) in the United States, landscape architecture's involvement with hydropower tends to be limited to the realm of mitigation. The infrastructure is viewed as something destructive to the landscape, and so hydroelectric landscapes become an accidental by-product of the infrastructure itself – sometimes beautiful, sometimes odd, but never intentionally designed.

Hydropower is currently making a comeback in public debate in Switzerland. The idea of building new dams and raising existing ones is gaining momentum, bolstered by climate change, the energy transition, the renewal of contracts for water rights, and—from the perspective of hydropower—opportunities coming from glacial meltwater generated by a warming planet. However, the discussion of landscape architecture's role in shaping these facilities has moved little since the 1970s: landscape remains a passive background in hydropower, which in most cases has had little to do with landscape other than causing its destruction. The story of Lake Sihl in northeastern

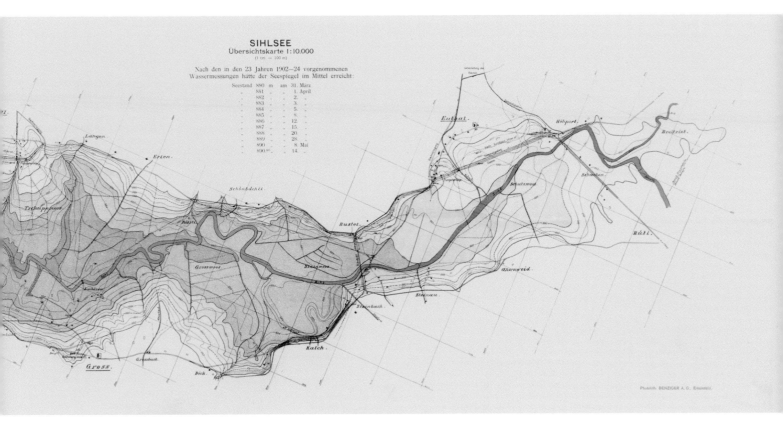

Switzerland challenges the assumed passive role of landscape in the formation of energy infrastructure; at the turn of the 20th century, a cohesive hydroelectric landscape was designed and engineered to be *beautiful*.[1] As evidenced by several clues in its conception–an artistic rendering, the engineering and regulation of its water levels, and the careful planting of its edges– there was an actual landscape architecture for this reservoir, and it was central to the infrastructural project of hydropower.

Lake Sihl is a reservoir located in northeastern Switzerland and part of the Etzelwerk hydroelectric complex. Its story starts in the late 19th century, as the Maschinenfabrik Oerlikon (MFO), one of Zurich's main industrial companies, was searching for new sources of energy to fuel its operations. In 1897, the company commissioned the firm of Swiss hydraulic engineer Louis Kürsteiner to determine a suitable site for a new hydropower facility. Kürsteiner proposed to build a hydropower plant in the Upper Sihl Valley and in the same year, the MFO submitted the project to the cantonal authorities. The proposal was based on the construction of two modest dams, 33 and 15 meters tall, that would form an extensive reservoir covering the entire valley floor. Water from the reservoir would then be brought by a conveyance pipe to a power plant by Lake Zurich, six kilometers further north and 400 meters lower in altitude. It then took 40 years of intense negotiation, and a transfer of the project from the MFO company

to the Swiss Federal Railway, to make it a reality: construction started in 1932 and ended in 1937. Today, the project rarely appears in histories and highlights of Swiss hydropower, as it features neither a record-breaking large dam nor a major technological innovation. It did, however, set two records in Swiss hydropower: the flooding of 11 square kilometers of land and the evacuation of about 2,000 inhabitants, making it the largest reservoir in Switzerland by surface, and the one that required the largest resettlement scheme.

The landscape of Switzerland's largest reservoir started taking shape in early debates about the project well before construction. Understandably, the project triggered a strong opposition, but there was also local support, owing to the poor condition of the Upper Sihl Valley before the Etzelwerk project. The valley floor suffered harsh weather conditions and possessed water-clogged and nutrient-poor soils that generally limited agriculture to straw cultivation and peat extraction, and as a result, the inhabitants of the valley were economically disadvantaged and faced high levels of unemployment. The economic outlook was so bleak that local farming corporations financially supported those among their members willing to move to the United States in hope of a better future.[2] In this context, the Etzelwerk project triggered resistance and interest simultaneously: the livelihoods of somewere threatened, while for others, hopes for a better

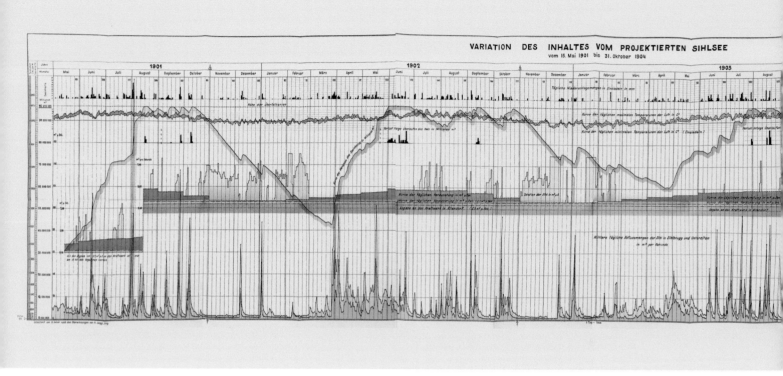

future were ignited. In debates between these opposing views, the proposed landscape of the hydro-electric facility featured heavily. A reservoir of this size was unprecedented in Switzerland at the time, and so the future landscape of Lake Sihl became a terrain of experimentation, and a prototype for this new type of hydroelectric landscape.

The first clue as to the aesthetic invention of Lake Sihl's landscape lies in an artist's rendering made in 1900. Its author, R. Wydler from the neighboring town of Einsiedeln, used a mixed technique of black ink, aquarelle, and gouache to frame a view to the south of the valley from an existing site. In the foreground, an agrarian scene, with buildings that still exist today; in the middle ground, a large lake that softly meets the mountain flanks and its villages; in the background, a circus of mountains, dominated by the snowy peaks of the Drüsberg chain. While the setting is idyllic at first sight, it hides a radical proposal. In the drawing, the lake appears as a natural lake would, its dam nowhere to be seen. The entire visual composition follows the archetypal scheme of mountains and lakes in the Alpine genre, which had already been practiced by influential artists both from Alpine countries, exemplified in the depictions of Lake Geneva by Swiss painters Ferdinand Hodler and Gustave Courbet, as well as by foreign visitors, as in J. M. W. Turner's paintings of Lake Zug and John Ruskin's drawing of the Dent d'Oche. A product of the romantic era, this genre allows for what scholar Michael Jakob terms a "double valorization" of

the landscape: mountains trigger a sense of the sublime with their verticality and imposing mass, while the calmly undulating shores of the lake offer an utterly picturesque setting.[3] The genre itself is an intersection of two larger aesthetic shifts that had been underway since the enlightenment: the aesthetic reinvention of mountains and water bodies. The Alps are the paradigmatic case for mountains: what was once a landscape of fear and danger–the Romans named the Alpine range *montes horribilis*–progressively became viewed as a place of pleasure and intrigue. This complete change in perception largely owed to the influence of English travelers fleeing the effects of industrialization on their domestic landscapes and finding an object of aesthetic and physical appreciation in the Alps. Over the same time span, a similar shift took place relative to landscapes of water. The ocean and its shore, long viewed as sites of danger and disgust, become a site of leisurely and artistic attention. By the time of the Romantic era, this shift in perception had extended from expansive coastal shorelines to smaller, inland water bodies, making lakes a new, ideal subject.

Wydler's painting directly adopts these pictorial traditions. Where it innovates, however, is its application to a human-made lake. By taking on the pictorial genre of Alpine lakes to represent a reservoir, the message is clear: the future Lake Sihl is just as entitled to beauty as any natural Alpine lake. The painting thereby performs two key actions: first, it naturalizes the reservoir,

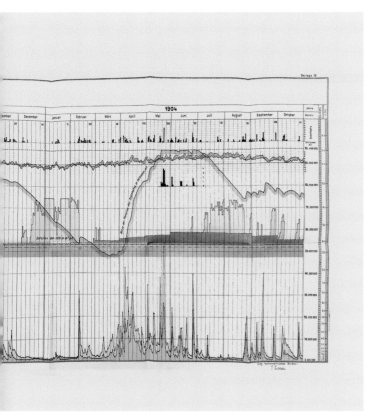

1 "Landscape" is understood here as the interplay of a site's material condition, perception, and cultural construction, drawing from the positions of Denis Cosgrove and W. J. T. Mitchell.

2 From 1850 to 1950, over 3,000 inhabitants relocated, most of whom settled in Louisville, Kentucky, USA, forming a "Schweizer Community" that still holds strong relations to the region of Einsiedeln today. See Susann Bosshard-Kälin, "Präsenz eines Schweizer Dorfes in der US-Stadt Louisville," *SWI swissinfo.ch* (July 5, 2016).

3 Michael Jakob, "L'invention du Léman," in Michael Jakob (ed.), *Autour du Léman: histoire et esthétique d'un espace lacustre* (MétisPresses, 2018), 16.

4 The poem in question is local poet Meinrad Lienert's *Sihlsee*. An example of a scientific report with aesthetic appreciation can be found in the summary of the report of health expert Dr. Wyss, who qualifies the Etzelwerk as "an essential embellishment," in Bezirksrat Einsiedeln, *Elektrizitätswerk am Etzel mit der Seeanlage im Hinterthal: Bericht und Anträge des Bezirksrates Einsiedeln* (Eberle & Rickenbach, 1900), 26. See also the lengthy digression of natural scientist Max Düggeli in his dissertation *Pflanzengeographische und wirtschaftliche Monographie des Sihltales bei Einsiedeln von Roblosen bis Studen (Gebiet des projektierten Sihlsees)* (Zürcher & Furrer, 1903), 3–4.

5 Bezirksrat Einsiedeln, *Bericht und Antrag des Bezirksrates Einsiedeln über die Etzelwerkkonzession* (Meinrad Ochsner, Buch und Akzidenzdruckerei, 1926), 23–24.

6 Bezirk Einsiedeln, "Neue Etzelwerkkonzession," https://www.einsiedeln.ch/verwaltung/laufende-projekte/neue-etzelwerkkonzession (accessed May 9, 2022).

7 The landscape architect Fritz Klauser designed a plantation scheme for the much smaller reservoir of Lake Gübsen near St. Gallen in 1930, but his involvement resulted of the concern of a local association 30 years after the completion of the reservoir. See P. Zülli, "A Storage Lake May Be Beautiful Too," *Anthos: Zeitschrift Für Landschaftsarchitektur* 3, no. 1 (1964).

8 Hans Nussbaumer, "Lake Sihl," *Anthos: Zeitschrift für Landschaftsarchitektur* 3, no. 1 (1964): 33.

suggesting how the landscape of Lake Sihl will conform to that of a natural lake, forming a landscape that is in no way wounded by its radical transformation, but rather enhanced with a new quality; and second, it transforms Lake Sihl from a technical requirement of the hydroelectric infrastructure into an object of desire. Beyond Wydler's painting, many other works contributed to the invention of this unprecedented landscape concept, including paintings, a poem written by the local poet Meinrad Lienert and sung by a local choir, newspaper articles that praised the Etzelwerk's landscape qualities, and even scientists—called in for their expertise in plants, human health, and economy—who authored reports citing benefits of the aesthetic improvement that would be brought by Lake Sihl.[4]

The absence of a dam in Wydler's painting is not the only way in which the human-made nature of the lake is hidden. The painting depicts a lake with water neatly meeting a lush shoreline. Yet, unlike most large natural lakes in Switzerland, hydroelectric reservoirs see their water levels fluctuate up to dozens of meters throughout the year. That is the direct consequence of their *raison d'être* – to store water and make it available at times of need. The case was no different for Lake Sihl. Early engineering calculations by Kürsteiner projected a variation up to 10 meters throughout the year: high from June to October, and progressively lowering until April, then rising again with the snowmelt. Wydler's painting therefore depicted one moment of the year when the water was high. When the water level dropped, another landscape

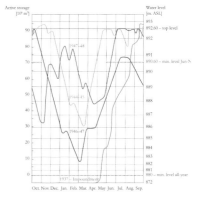

Above: Water levels of Lake Sihl measured in the years 1937, 1944-45, 1946-47, and 1947-48. The horizontal red lines indicate the water level fixed for the summer months.

was formed: part of the lakebed would be revealed, forming a different shoreline, mineral in its materiality, devoid of vegetation, displaying shades from gray to brown. The result was closer to a desert or the surface of the moon than to the picturesque shore of a romantic Alpine lake.

Consequently, as the project neared construction, the commission preparing the contracts introduced a new clause. With a maximum water level of 892.60 meters, the clause set a minimum water level of 880 meters throughout the year, and of 890.60 meters from the first of June to the first of November each year.[5] Should the facility operator not meet these conditions, it would be fined for each day the water remained below the required level. As such, the water level could be expected to remain high in the summer months, just as in Wydler's painting. The measure was presented as a sanitary one, yet this sanitary umbrella is remarkably large, including other measures such as a requirement to plant the shoreline and to preserve the landscape image of the valley to the greatest possible extent. Whether or not landscape aesthetics were an implicit motivation of this clause, the motivation has become explicit today. The contracts for water rights have reached the end of their validity and are currently being re-negotiated. In this process, the commission preparing the contracts has already announced that it will hold on to the regulation of the water level, "for sentimental reasons" and to preserve the landscape's image.[6] The regulation of fluctuation thus shifted from a sanitary concern to an aesthetic and experiential one. Through this action, the form and temporality of Lake Sihl was steered in a specific direction. Fluctuation control was no longer purely a question of engineering, but a design tool to make Lake Sihl conform to Wydler's original image, at least in the summer months.

Around 1940, a second effort was made to shape the landscape of Lake Sihl into Wydler's vision. The facility operator commissioned the Mertens brothers–a prominent Swiss landscape architecture practice at the time–to design a planting scheme for the shoreline, in what was possibly the first case of landscape architectural involvement in a reservoir project in Switzerland.[7] Their scheme followed a resolutely picturesque approach, whose prime concern was the spatial experience along the shore and the careful framing of views. They proposed to plant "individual as well as groups of woods on the new banks of the lake, so that, seen from the new shore-road, the foreground was filled out and, framing the landscape in the distance, gave it depth. The dead stripe left at low water level could thus, at least partially, be banned from the field of vision and not offend any more in its entirety."[8] Drawing from an extensive heritage of landscape design for the shores of water bodies, there was little conceptual novelty in their parti to articulate spaces and frame views along the shoreline. However, inasmuch as their approach sought to frame views, it also sought to obscure them by diminishing the visual impact of the empty lakebed and amplifying the idyllic vision contained in Wydler's image.

Lake Sihl was neither just an accidental result nor simply beautified after construction, but rather was *invented* as something beautiful.

Instead of remaining limited by a pessimistic understanding of mitigating a damaged natural landscape, the case of Lake Sihl demonstrates how the scope of landscape and aesthetics can widen to address not only the challenges presented by implementing new energy infrastructures, but also the imagination of potential qualities that can emerge within these landscapes. Understanding the integral role of landscape and aesthetics in the case of Lake Sihl allows us to rethink the question of landscape in hydropower, and energy infrastructures more broadly.

The aesthetic invention of this hydroelectric landscape suggests that new aesthetic constructions for infrastructure are not only possible, but can also become powerful enough to question the basis of aesthetic preconceptions that "natural" beauty is "appropriate," and thus open up possibilities for new and novel aesthetics and experiences. While the Mertens brothers' planting scheme demonstrates how traditional conventions in landscape architecture can offer solutions to new problems, it also begs the question of what might have been possible were they able to design free from the picturesque vision laid out in Wydler's artwork. The regulation of water levels, too, was bound by this initial image in order to produce a certain idealized landscape in which low water was seen as negative. However, at times of low water, locals have found that in the shallow parts of the lakebed, the old roads that once crossed the valley emerge once again. These temporary paths offer new ways to move through the valley, and to relate to former ways of life through the roads people once routinely traveled. These poetic and playful moments are purely accidental, but suggest the potential to recast low water as a positive, ephemeral moment wholly integrated into the life and experience of this invented landscape. It is up to landscape architects to cultivate these novel qualities within hybrid landscapes, and to stake an intentional position in the implementation and aesthetic invention of hydropower and other renewable energy infrastructures.

WINIFRED CURRAN, MICHELLE STUHLMACHER + ELSA ANDERSON
GETTING TO JUST GREEN ENOUGH

Winifred Curran is a professor of geography at DePaul University in Chicago. She is the author of *Gender and Gentrification* (2018) and coeditor, with Trina Hamilton, of *Just Green Enough: Urban Development and Environmental Gentrification* (2018).

Michelle Stuhlmacher is an assistant professor of geography at DePaul University. Her research employs satellite imagery to measure green space and its social and environmental impacts on urban systems.

Elsa Anderson is an assistant professor of instruction at Northwestern University, Illinois, and an affiliate scientist at the Chicago Botanic Garden, where she leads the Chicago Biodiversity Project. Her expertise is in urban social-ecological systems and plant ecology, and particularly connecting people with the other species that live in cities.

+ PLANNING, ENVIRONMENTAL JUSTICE

Where we choose to see beauty in the urban landscape shapes urban development. Some understand the gentrification of urban neighborhoods through the economic concept of the "beauty contest,"[1] in which our understanding of a neighborhood is shaped by what we believe other people think about that place. One powerful tool in shaping this perception is the proliferation of expensive greening projects in urban areas that have previously experienced disinvestment. This creates green gentrification, a process where new green investment spurs development that leads to an increase in real estate costs and, therefore, the displacement of long-term residents.[2]

Evidence clearly shows that greening in previously disinvested neighborhoods can lead to gentrification. The most famous example is New York's High Line, a rails-to-trails park that raised property values in the surrounding area by 103%.[3] In Chicago, the 606 rails-to-trails project raised surrounding property values by 48%,[4] and Atlanta's BeltLine project increased property values up to 26%.[5] This leads marginalized communities to be wary of new green space projects, worried they will have to choose between greening and affordability.[6] We describe the fight in one historically underserved Chicago neighborhood, Pilsen, to learn from these examples by working to accomplish measurable environmental improvements in ways that are impactful for current residents without being "beautiful" enough to further spur gentrification.

The legacy of uneven development and racial segregation in American cities has led to a profound "green gap" that "emerges when land deemed vacant, underused, or contaminated is identified by developers as a possible area to be 'greened,' generating amenities that may allow for higher economic value and profit accumulation."[7] In other words, today's green opportunities *require* disinvested landscapes and thus build upon and reinforce existing socioeconomic and racial inequalities. In realizing the "green gap," projects intended to improve environmental outcomes reinforce and exacerbate conditions that further inequity, marginalization, and displacement. Too rarely do these projects start with an equity lens and include concrete measures for ensuring that greening solutions benefit all residents.

To counter green gentrification that exploits this "green gap," Curran and Hamilton suggested the "just green enough" strategy,[8] which aims to forestall green gentrification by engaging in community-led greening initiatives that prioritize meaningful environmental justice improvements over aesthetics. There are many ways to be green and to find beauty in the urban landscape beyond a highly curated park. The just green enough approach argues that that which appears green and beautiful may not necessarily be the most environmentally impactful. Instead, focusing on meeting the needs of residents and improving their environmental outcomes will lead to more substantive environmental improvements and decouple green space provision from high-end real estate development. The just green enough approach finds and enhances beauty in unexpected places, celebrating the resilience of existing natures and communities.[9]

A central tenet of the just green enough approach is that it is not a one-size-fits-all prescription but rather an approach that centers democratic community engagement to achieve substantive environmental improvements. There are many ways to be "just green enough" to improve the environment without necessarily stimulating gentrification. We explore what a just green enough approach looks like in the Pilsen neighborhood of Chicago, where activists, faced with a proposed rails-to-trails project called El Paseo, are trying to repair a century of pollution without further spurring gentrification as was experienced by other predominantly Latinx communities along Chicago's 606 trail.

The Case of the 606

Many existing projects aimed at beautifying previously derelict spaces are built upon existing racial and economic inequalities. The 606 trail in Chicago, an elevated rails-to-trails project that runs through four gentrified and gentrifying neighborhoods, is one such example. While originally a community-initiated idea, the 606 has become an instrument of gentrification and displacement. Implementation of the project was transferred from the City of Chicago to the non-profit Trust for Public Land. Despite the obvious speculative pressures a large-scale green infrastructure project like this would exert in the historically disinvested neighborhoods that surrounded the site, the city did nothing to preserve affordable housing or enact any concrete initiatives to curb displacement until a year after the trail opened. Attempts by community activists to address the affordability and displacement issues were stonewalled, with the city referring residents to the Trust for Public Land for anything related to the 606, and the Trust for Public Land telling residents, rightly, that "We are not in the business of housing." The results were substantial increases in property values and median rent.[10]

The fear is that clearing space for greening projects such as these is less about improving green space accessibility and "more about removing unwanted people and activities in order to prime the sites for economic gain."[11] While the creation of these types of spaces is often part of an argument to improve neighborhoods and achieve more sustainable

urban development, these arguments can ring hollow. Projects like the 606, with their paved paths, are unlikely to be more environmentally friendly than the "rot" they replace; construction and maintenance of these park sites is energy intensive, polluting, and expensive.[12] With the 606 as the poster child for large-scale green space development and community revitalization in Chicago, community activists in Pilsen have sought to follow a different model.

Pilsen and El Paseo

Pilsen, a Latinx, predominantly Mexican, community on the southwest side of Chicago, is underserved by green space and faces significant environmental justice challenges.[13] Pilsen is overburdened with environmental hazards, including air quality concerns and soil contamination from both current and legacy industrial sites. The Pilsen Industrial Corridor along the Chicago River serves as the southern boundary of the neighborhood. This concentration of industry was historically a reliable source of jobs to new immigrants, who also suffered the effects of its pollution. Until 2012, Pilsen was home to the Fisk coal-burning power plant. Nationwide, the Fisk plant was second only to the Crawford Power Plant (in the adjacent Little Village neighborhood) for its pollutant emissions and environmental justice risks to communities of color. Together, the Fisk and Crawford plants were estimated to cause 41 deaths, 500 emergency room visits, and 2,800 asthma attacks each year.[14] The EPA has conducted remediation efforts at numerous sites to address soil lead contamination and is continuing to work on improving Pilsen's air quality. In 2013, the EPA and the State of Illinois signed a consent decree with H. Kramer—a firm with a brass smelting foundry located across the street from a Pilsen elementary school—to resolve violations of the Clean Air Act and state air pollution laws. The EPA is currently assessing the degree to which another industrial business in the area, Sims Metal Management, a metal shredder and recycling facility, is in compliance with the Clean Air Act after Sims was sued by the Illinois Attorney General for violating air pollution laws. Sims is within a mile of three neighborhood schools, and their permit is up for renewal. The community is strongly opposed to granting a renewed permit (more on this later).

As a neighborhood that is also experiencing gentrification, there is concern that greening will accelerate increasing housing prices and the displacement of long-term residents.[15] One central area of concern is the proposed El Paseo rails-to-trails project a 4.2-mile-long, at grade multi-use greenway proposed by the City of Chicago in 2016 that would run along the now unused BNSF rail line. The trail would incorporate El Paseo Community Garden. The City's plan is for the trail to be managed by the community, citing El Paseo Community

Garden's management through the NeighborSpace nonprofit urban land trust as the model.[16] While plans for the trail are currently stalled, due largely to safety concerns about having cyclists and pedestrians concentrated in an area so heavy with truck traffic and pollution, it continues to spark residents' fears that it will accelerate gentrification in parts of the neighborhood.

There is already evidence of this. Even though the trail does not yet exist (though train tracks have been removed and the soil remediated along sections of the route), real estate listings advertise units as being on the trail and have incorporated pictures of the garden space in anticipation that this will boost property values.[18] In this way, the neighborhood's fight for environmental justice and housing justice is linked. In 2019, voters in the area passed a nonbinding referendum, with over 90 percent of the vote, calling for a community benefits agreement for El Paseo that would require 30 percent affordable housing for any new housing projects along the trail, a property tax freeze, and city funding for local jobs and affordable housing. Pilsen residents are all too aware of the effect of the 606 on housing prices and want to avoid the same fate in their neighborhood. As one organizer put it, "This is an opportunity for us to think big. We know something is coming...but this is our chance to say, 'What if? What if you build affordable housing with it?'"[19] There is the recognition that, while Pilsen does need more green space, gentrification is the most important issue in the community. Whatever greening does occur, it must be developed within a social justice framework that aims to repair decades of harm, rather than further marginalize long-term residents. As the neighborhood's progressive alderman says, "We want to create a model that works."[20]

While this process of trying to create a new model of urban greening is still very much in progress, there are some important lessons to take away from Pilsen's work to be "just green enough." One is that the community wants to see genuine progress toward cleaning up pollution rather than prioritizing beautiful new green space – in other words, to "clean before green." Parks like the 606 or the proposed El Paseo present the useful illusion that green space development is making cities more sustainable, but what is their real environmental impact, especially compared to other strategies that cities could, but rarely do, enact, such as regulating environmental polluters?[21]

Community activists from the Southwest Environmental Alliance and other community groups called on public officials to do just that in an April 2022 meeting about the renewal of the Sims permit attended by around 400 people. Elected representatives and representatives from the City Department

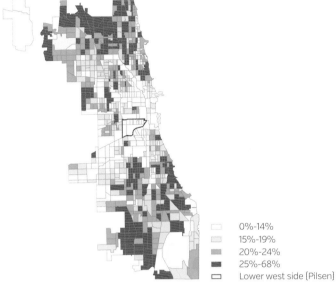

0%-14%
15%-19%
20%-24%
25%-68%
Lower west side (Pilsen)

Tree density in Chicago

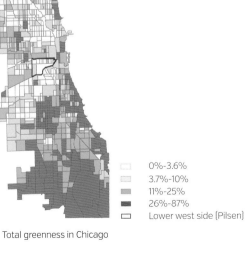

0%-3.6%
3.7%-10%
11%-25%
26%-87%
Lower west side (Pilsen)

Total greenness in Chicago

1 Erica Barnett & Ben Klemens, "The Beauty Contest: How cities are shaped by what we think others think [Part I]," *Strong Towns* (November 6, 2018).

2 Melissa Checker, "Wiped Out by the 'Greenwave': Environmental Gentrification and the Paradoxical Politics of Urban Sustainability," *City & Society* 23, no.2 (2012): 210–29.

3 Mihir Zaveri & Daniel Slotnik, "$60 Million High Line Expansion to Connect Park to Moynihan Train Hall." *New York Times*, January 11, 2021.

4 Geoff Smith et al., "Measuring the Impact of The 606: Understanding How a Large Public Investment Impacted the Surrounding Housing Market" (DePaul University: Institute for Housing Studies, 2016), https://www.housingstudies.org/media/filer_public/2016/10/31/ihs_measuring_the_impact_of_the_606.pdf.

5 Dan Immergluck & Tharunya Balan, "Sustainable for Whom? Green Urban Development, Environmental Gentrification, and the Atlanta Beltline," *Urban Geography* 39, no. 4 (2018): 546–62.

6 Checker, "Wiped Out by the 'Greenwave,'" 211.

7 Isabelle Anguelovski, James Connolly & Anna Livia Brand, "From Landscapes of Utopia to the Margins of the Green Urban Life," *City* 22, no.3 (2018): 417–36.

8 Winifred Curran & Trina Hamilton, "Just Green Enough: Contesting Environmental Gentrification in Greenpoint, Brooklyn." *Local Environment* 17, no. 9 (2012): 1027–42; Winifred Curran & Trina Hamilton (eds), *Just Green Enough: Urban Development and Environmental Gentrification* (Routledge, 2017).

9 A good example of this is the Newtown Creek Nature Walk, see Winifred Curran & Trina Hamilton, "Nature-based Solutions in Hiding: Goslings and greening in the still-industrial city," *Socio-Ecological Practice Research 2*, no. 4 (2020), 321–27.

10 Smith et al., "Measuring the Impact of the 606," ibid.

11 Kevin Loughran, *Parks for Profit: Selling Nature in the City* (Columbia University Press, 2022), 182.

12 Ibid.

13 Michelle Stuhlmacher, Yushim Kim & Ji Eun Kim, "The Role of Green Space in Chicago's Gentrification," *Urban Forestry & Urban Greening* 71 (May 2022).

14 NAACP, Indigenous Environmental Network and LVEJO, *Coal Blooded: Putting Profits Before People* (2012), https://naacp.org/resources/coal-blooded-putting-profits-people.

15 Heather Cherone & Mauricio Peña, "Pilsen, Little Village Voters Tell City Officials El Paseo Needs A Community Benefits Agreement," *BlockClub Chicago* (March 4, 2019).

16 El Paseo Trail, https://elpaseotrail.org/faq/.

of Public Health, the Illinois EPA, and the regional administrator of the EPA were called upon to individually affirm their commitment to work toward a cumulative health impacts study for Pilsen and to use their power to achieve measurable improvements in Pilsen's environment within the next two years. Each representative, in turn, made these commitments. Activists also called for a permit moratorium during the length of any health study. The city had announced just prior to the meeting that they would conduct a citywide health study on the effects of pollution on Chicagoans as part of a bigger program to spend pandemic relief funds on environmental justice and climate preparedness efforts.[22] This followed new data from the City showing that Chicago's Latinx residents saw a more than three-year drop in life expectancy between 2019 and 2020–the steepest decline for any group–and have lost a total of seven years of life expectancy since 2012.[23]

With such deeply racialized health disparities and geographies of pollution, the first step for any claim to greening or sustainability in Pilsen must be led by measurable environmental improvements that may not be visible as "green"or accomplish beautification of the landscape but are critical for long-term residents to feel safe in their neighborhood. Any green interventions that are not directly predicated on remediating and reversing the area's toxic legacy are clearly not aimed at the existing community. Research has shown that if perceptions of environmental injustice linger, they will impact usage, despite whatever urban greening transformation is occurring.[24] Green without clean is aimed at gentrifiers, who have not had to suffer decades of pollution and illness and who worry less about long-term health consequences because they are transitory and will typically be in the neighborhood only a few years.

While Pilsen does have a documented history of environmental injustice, we must be careful not to equate it with a divested wasteland in need of saving by gentrifiers. Pilsen is beautiful, with historic architecture and a rich cultural history and legacy of activism to celebrate. To highlight some of the neighborhood's unique aspects, namely its rich tradition of street murals, some in the community have suggested an alternative site for El Paseo, along 16th St at the northern boundary of the neighborhood, rather than on Sangamon Street as currently proposed. A greening project along 16th St would be welcome, since residents have long complained about the lack of upkeep along the rail viaduct on 16th St, with issues ranging from falling concrete to pigeon waste, even as the viaduct hosts a wide array of celebrated murals. The hope is that the slightly more peripheral location might be less of a speculative trigger than the current site and help to

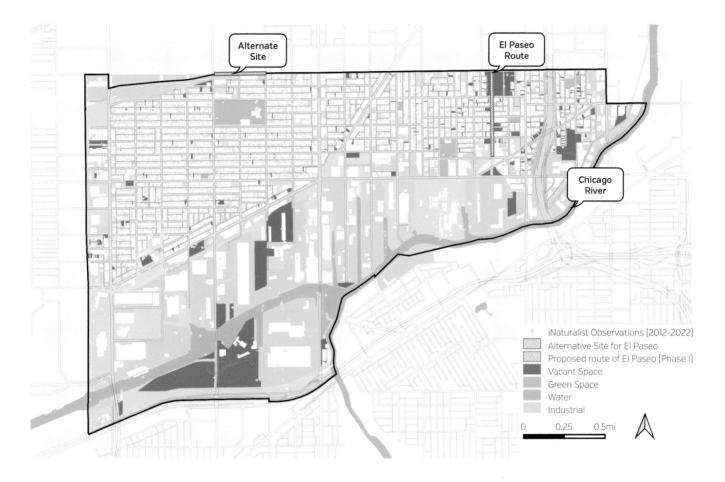

Alternate Site

El Paseo Route

Chicago River

- iNaturalist Observations (2012-2022)
- Alternative Site for El Paseo
- Proposed route of El Paseo (Phase I)
- Vacant Space
- Green Space
- Water
- Industrial

0   0.25   0.5mi

highlight an area of the neighborhood of which residents are rightly proud. At the time of writing, meetings to discuss this possibility were being planned.[25]

Similarly, while Pilsen is underserved by green space and overburdened by pollution, that does not mean there are no environmental features to celebrate. Recent work in partnership with the Chicago Botanic Garden to track biodiversity in the area through community involvement via the iNaturalist app has revealed over 200 species of plants and animals in Pilsen. While many of these species are common in urban areas, information about specific species profiles provides valuable insight into the types of nature that already exist in Pilsen and allows us to examine and communicate the roles of existing biodiversity. For example, common species in Pilsen, such as the common sunflower and the Norway maple, have relatively high soil purification and air filtration capacities, even though they are not typical species included in greening

projects. Furthermore, the greatest concentrations of these observations of biodiversity are not in existing parks or the more gentrified segments of the neighborhood, but along the industrial corridor, where vacant space allows many species to thrive. Overall, data from iNaturalist reminds us that nature and biodiversity exist even in neighborhoods like Pilsen where formal green space is limited and development is a major concern. Indeed, a just green enough method for Pilsen might center on embracing these bits of nature that already exist in vacant lots and other peripheral spaces as a canvas for targeted improvements in infrastructure (e.g., adding benches or mulched trails) or the presence of symbiotic species (e.g., planting pollinator gardens).

Conclusion

Rather than celebrating only the green that is aesthetically pleasing, curated, and well-manicured (and expensive), planner and preservationist Daniel Campo argues instead that, "Achieving

balance between the designed and the undesigned in perhaps a hybrid form of public space has the potential to provide more cost-effective options than the expensive parks that are now championed by urban leadership." Cities need another form of "nature that is more flexible, pliable, open, and available on a more ad hoc basis."[26] The open and industrial spaces of Pilsen provide this opportunity to be part of the solution rather than just reifying Pilsen as an environmental sacrifice zone. How could we think more creatively about accomplishing measurable environmental improvements building upon needed remediation and purification rather than limiting our imagination of what green looks like to another rails-to-trails project?

Activists in Pilsen are organizing with an explicit racial justice lens to accomplish greener, more equitable urban futures. They have linked affordable housing to the provision of green space through a ballot referendum, used public pressure to demand accountability from both industry and their public representatives, insisted on a transparent and democratic process to identify and repair the host of environmental ills to which longtime residents have been subjected and worked toward a more democratic process to recognize and celebrate the beauty that is special to Pilsen rather than submitting to sparkly green projects designed and administered from above. A just green enough approach requires a much more substantive and expansive view of how to be "green," one that foregrounds measurable environmental improvements over that which looks pretty and forces us to confront the unjust outcomes of traditional greening projects.

17 Madison Savedra," Proposed El Paseo trail on hold, southwest side aldermen say," *BlockClub Chicago* [May 3, 2022].

18 Chicago's Property Shop, "Pilsen Apartments Near the Paseo Trail" [May 18, 2022], https://www.chicagospropertyshop.com/chicago/apartments-near-paseo-trail/; Patty Wetli, "Pilsen's El Paseo Community Garden Hedges Against Gentrification with Half-Acre Expansion," *WTTW* [October 21, 2020].

19 Quoted in Cherone & Peña, ibid.

20 Ibid.

21 Loughran, *Parks for Profit*, ibid., 135.

22 Brett Chase, "City announces big environmental impact study as Pilsen residents protest metal shredder," *Chicago Sun-Times* [April 27, 2022].

23 City of Chicago, Office of the Mayor, "Life Expectancy in Chicago Declined During the Pandemic's First Year with the Biggest Drops Among Black and Latinx Chicagoans," press release [April 25, 2022].

24 David Kelly et al., "Urban greening for health and wellbeing in low-income communities: A baseline study in Melbourne, Australia," *Cities* 120 no. 1 [2022].

25 Savedra, "Proposed El Paseo trail on hold," ibid.

26 Daniel Campo, *The Accidental Playground: Brooklyn Waterfront Narratives of the Undesigned and Unplanned* [Fordham University Press, 2013]: 252.

Opposite, Top: Proposed route of El Paseo trail along Sangamon Street.

Opposite, Bottom: Murals along 16th Street, the proposed alternate route of El Paseo trail.

BLACKNESS AND BEAUTY
IN CONVERSATION WITH BRANDI THOMPSON SUMMERS

Brandi Thompson Summers is an associate professor of geography at the University of California, Berkeley, and is author of *Black in Place: The Spatial Aesthetics of Race in a Post-Chocolate City* (2019). Her research examines the relationship between and function of race, space, urban infrastructure, and architecture. Summers has published both in scholarly and popular publications, including *New York Times*, *The Boston Globe*, *Antipode*, and *Places Journal*. She was interviewed for this issue by planner and architect **Libby Viera-Bland**, Director of Neighborhood Development at Project Row Houses, where she focuses on long-term strategies to build affordable housing and support neighborhood preservation in Houston, Texas's Third Ward.

+ As Black women in urban design professions, I think that we have a unique perspective on how we look at beauty and what beauty means in different contexts. I'm very excited to hear your input. Let's start with a big question: how do you define beauty? Who or what is the most beautiful to you?

As it relates to my work, I am focused more on the behavior that comes from our understanding of beauty – what is built into various social and political structures, and how we understand taste and who determines it. I think beauty and behavior are connected, and I don't think that beauty is necessarily entirely positive or negative. Personally, what I find to be beautiful are things that make me think, things that make me wonder, and things that make me feel good. That's why I do appreciate and love design. Sometimes it's the one space where I feel like I don't have to follow a trend; I don't necessarily have to explain why I like something – just the simple fact that I do is what matters the most.

In my work, I'm mostly preoccupied with Blackness, though that doesn't mean that it's always attributed to Black people. I do believe that there are ways in which cultural producers who shape something based upon their own experience—or perhaps based upon certain limitations or opportunities—can create something beautiful and interesting. But again, for me personally, beauty is what's most stimulating.

I think it's not necessarily something that happens along a psychological process. I think there's a way that the connection, or at least meaning connected to Blackness, needs to be broken in order to justify its ability to be consumed by others. So, you don't explicitly say something is Black to encourage someone to consume it, to buy it, to eat it, to smell it, to live in it, to live by it.

You mentioned the word authenticity and of course that's a fraught term. What ends up being real is oftentimes artifice, and it's something that needs to be imbued with meaning, usually by those who are in power. So I think there is a process—if we think about the material world, if we think about the built environment or structures—where there has to be this break in the link to Black people in order for it to be more general, despite the fact that we may know this feels like something that is attributed to Black people because the assumption is anything that's urban is Black. We still make that kind of connection. We make that connection specifically in the United States, and that's from a longer history. It doesn't come from nowhere; it's not based on a particular claim. It is based on various structural manifestations where Black people were relegated to particular parts of a city. So if we think about this as it relates to cultural production, I am certain that there is a both intentional and unintentional way in which the signifier has to be made empty in order to fill it up with these other meanings that people need to either sell or fully commodify this particular understanding of race and specifically Blackness.

+ Building on that thought, when we think about cities we often think about people striving for an "authentic" urban living experience in terms of culture and aesthetics. And what we know about urbanity is that typically those aesthetics are pretty explicitly Black in their foundations and influences. The more desirable those elements become, the more likely we know Black people are to be displaced from those communities. At what point do we start to think of urban aesthetics as being an empty signifier, as having lost their meaning?

+ Continuing that thought pattern around commodification, there tends to be a pretty voyeuristic fetishization of Black beauty, especially with respect to Black women and spaces like the ghetto by white audiences. As a result, we see Black bodies and spaces consumed via an external lens from a safe distance without regard for the lived experience. How do we contemplate the line between observing something or admiring it as beautiful versus fetishizing it?

I want to take a step back because I think that particular perspective still prioritizes and privileges the perspective of a white gaze. And I don't. In my writing and in my thinking, I'm not trying to think about that. Instead, I'm trying to locate what I already know exists, but often doesn't get enough attention. So while there is this fetishization of Black beauty, Black beauty is multidimensional and diverse, so there isn't necessarily one particular idea of Black beauty, despite the fact that you'll find that various institutions will attempt to narrow the definition of Black beauty, or at least contain this particular image of what is beautiful and what is Black.

And so I think in a way, yes, there is this external commodified version of Black beauty that does get replicated and that does become reproduced in various locations and that is what is being observed. That's what is being consumed. That's what is being commodified, rather than what I find to be beautiful about Black culture or about Black productivity, Black labor, Black homes, Black space, Black everything. So that line between admiration and fetishization ends up becoming more based on white fetishization rather than what relates specifically to Black people. I think we should interrogate that rather than thinking about what makes up Black beauty, or at least the epidermalization of Blackness that ends up being consumed by white people.

Sure, but also there's this nagging thing about representation – that there's this need to represent people in particular ways, and oftentimes those are the aestheticized ways of showing or demonstrating that people exist in a particular location. I find it's more a case of Blackness-as-object standing in for the actual subject, and that in itself is enough for a lot of locations, cities, neighborhoods, to say that they are offering a wealth of resources and things that people need.

What ends up happening, as it relates to beauty and connecting that to community or connecting that to people's quality of life aesthetics, is that the focus is on looking to culture rather than recognizing additional needs. So where you have disinvestment in particular communities where blight is determined, there are things in that community that are considered ugly, outdated, structurally unsound, etc. But those things need to be determined. You have to be told that your place is not habitable, right? Just saying, "Look, where I'm living is not safe" is often not enough for the state to actually respond and do anything about it.

Once those areas have been determined to be uninhabitable by various actors—private developers, local governments, state governments—you find that the replacement isn't one-to-one. It ends up being a lot less. And then on top of that, they may add some kind of cultural center or something. Again, that's related to representation rather than fulfilling the needs of the people who are there. So you see the ways that an emphasis on beauty or an emphasis on habitability ends up getting intertwined with people's needs and rather than meeting those needs, they instead fill up the beauty quotient when we might actually need real services and material goods.

+ I'm interested in the idea of fetishization and commodification and where it starts to relate to gentrification and disinvestment in Black neighborhoods and communities. Historically this can be attributed to the legacy of redlining, but I'm curious to hear your perspective on whether beauty is playing a role at all in the disinvestment in communities of color.

No. And I say that because when I've thought about aesthetics connected to beauty, I've used bell hooks's work to help shape my thinking rather than the philosophers that are most often discussed as we think about beauty and aesthetics and taste. There's this idea that Black people are not supposed to be able to produce something that's beautiful or even recognize something that's beautiful or certainly of value. As a result, she might find that her childhood home might not be described as beautiful based on these Eurocentric, wealthy perspectives, despite the fact that she can recognize the value and the aesthetic purchase that it has on her family, on herself, and others. I think that you don't necessarily have to define something as having more value than another, but instead see their utility. Something can become beautiful because it can be helpful, because it can make someone feel good, because it can make them feel safe–or, in the same way, be perceived as dangerous or make them feel unsafe–and so that's when it can become something else.

+ I think we can flip this question a little bit and look at it from a different perspective too. There are a lot of Black spaces that are not intended to be found beautiful for white Eurocentric audiences. They're not built within that lens. I'm thinking about Black rural communities, for example. Does your definition of beauty change in different physical or cultural environments?

+ I think that there's something to the relationship between Black aesthetics and the public performance of Black aesthetics: when we talk about–again, coming from that white lens–what's "ghetto," or gauche, or over-the-top, or too "hood" for public consumption or public display. I'm curious if you would talk a little bit about the relationship between Black aesthetics and public performance.

You know, that's something that I, many, many years ago, had intended to write more about, especially as it related to high fashion aesthetics when there was this move toward streetwear, which in a lot of ways was dependent on Black cultural shifts and representations of Black life, especially in New York, Chicago, Los Angeles, and other locations where there were significant Black populations.

There's something about the artifice again – the play that parodies the potential beauty that's there. I've written about the 2012 "Haute Mess" spread in *Vogue Italia*, where they took markers of not just opulence, as you think about the very expensive clothing items that they were wearing, but also markers of this kind of "debased culture." If we think about fast food, if we think about malt liquor, if we're thinking about acrylic nails and what was deemed tacky at the time or, like you said, "ghetto"– there were actually some acrylic toenails that were put on some of the models that had been called "ghe-toes." So, using those kinds of props, it creates this absurdity in the performance that in a lot of ways allows the white body to deny this kind of negative representation of Black culture because it's so over-the-top.

As it relates to performance, I think that how the body who is performing that particular act is racialized makes a huge difference in how it's consumed. Of course, we're seeing this in the TikTok dances and such, right? Where there are white creators who are making all kinds of money and receiving a lot of attention for essentially copying and stealing the work and labor of Black creators. And so we know the ways that Black bodies in terms of how they perform are devalued unless there is a white person who takes it up and perhaps even makes their own version of it. I think in terms of monetary value as it relates to whether someone's work actually is paid for, that's where we start to see that dynamic playing out. But as it relates to its legibility among Black folks, no. I still think there is incredible value to Black performance, whether we are performing ourselves within our community or not. It may not necessarily come in the form of money, but it certainly has value in terms of belonging, acceptance, and a variety of things that can make you feel good and connected to various communities.

+ When that TikTok protest happened right after "Thot Shit" by Megan Thee Stallion came out and Black TikTokers refused to make dances, it was fascinating to watch what unfolded with the white creators when there weren't any dances for them to copy from Black creators.

Exactly. And the thing is, there's actually an opportunity for the white creators to make fun or to even reproduce. They would make really drab performances, right? They wouldn't put any effort into it. So, if white creators actually parodied that, it would start a really interesting and dynamic conversation about this kind of theft that's occurring. But, you know, that would mean that they would have to acknowledge the fact that they're stealing, and they're not interested in doing that.

Yeah, you know, this is where representation ends up not being enough. So those are abysmal numbers. However, you'll see what happened after the racial reckoning in 2020 where there's an abundance of jobs, opportunities, or funding to essentially add some color to the mix without proper infrastructure to actually support those people and make sure they're successful. We don't want that. We certainly want people to have access to opportunities for sure. But on the other hand, as my friend Olalekan Jeyifous has said before, it's so clear that designers and architects in particular cannot feel as though they solve problems. They don't! And so part of it is, how do you reconcile that? How do you reconcile your belief that you're getting into this particular field in order to solve aesthetic and functional problems with the reality that there are so many structural burdens and inequities that can't be solved by design?

Recognizing that makes it really important to how designers approach different spaces. That means you're not always the expert when you try to build a world for everyone. Instead, it might mean that you have to be student more often than you are a teacher when you're producing something.

The other element is, I think, that architects and especially landscape architects are in a lot of ways trained not to think about people. You're thinking about the environment that of course is going to be used by people, but it's more so how to make spaces sustainable, which doesn't necessarily mean habitable. It doesn't necessarily mean that people–or too many people–should be in this space. How do we conceive of modernity, which is supposed to produce this permanence and structures that are to last for a long time, and couple that with a degradation of the environment because there are too many humans inhabiting a space?

There are all of these elements that architects and designers have to think about, and for so long it's actually marginalized communities that come up with the most sustainable ideas. So, if I were to think about these fields it's more so that you kind of have to blow it up. You have to unlearn a lot of what you've learned and recognize that training, especially if it's very Eurocentric and based very much on Enlightenment politics and ideologies that structure the field, is of a particular time. Then, you might be able to open the field up to think about other perspectives and other methods and other ways of knowing and seeing.

+ Coming back to that bell hooks reference, I think it was in *Art on My Mind* when she was telling the story of being in grade school and being told to draw her house, and the feeling that it inspired of wanting to become a designer, wanting to become an architect, and really starting to admire and analyze the spaces around her. Certainly, the landscape architectural and architectural professions in the United States are very explicitly dominated by white designers: 0.2% of landscape architects and 2% of architects are Black.[1] When you narrow the field down to Black women, the percentage falls to 0.4% of licensed architects.[2] Especially within the context of that bell hooks story, what would you want the design profession to take into account as they design spaces of beauty for a multiracial, intersectional public?

You know, it's funny because whenever I give talks at schools of architecture, planning departments, or adjacent fields I'm often thinking how much I really enjoy it, mostly because I see that there are so many limitations to how these fields really conceive of race, racialization, and the relationship to the built environment. I would more so encourage there to be increased interdisciplinarity to specifically landscape architecture, but also other related fields and subfields because oftentimes it's people like me, the newest geographers, who are particularly interested and invested in material conditions that produce the kinds of spaces that allow you to build in this natural environment that is no longer natural.

So, it's not really a question I wish you'd asked; I would just encourage thinking more interdisciplinarily about these issues, especially if we're going to try to co-construct a livable future for so many people.

+ Well, thank you so much. Those were all of my prepared questions. Is there a question that you wish that I had asked?

1 "Landscape Architect Demographics and Statistics in the U.S.," *Zippia* [Accessed March 3, 2023], https://www.zippia.com/landscape-architect-jobs/demographics/; "Design Architect Demographics and Statistics in the U.S.," *Zippia* [Accessed March 3, 2023], https://www.zippia.com/architect-jobs/demographics/.

2 Katherine Guimapang, "Number of Licensed Black Female Architects increasese to 500," *Archinect* [December 21, 2020], https://archinect.com/news/article/150233756/number-of-licensed-black-female-architects-increases-to-500.

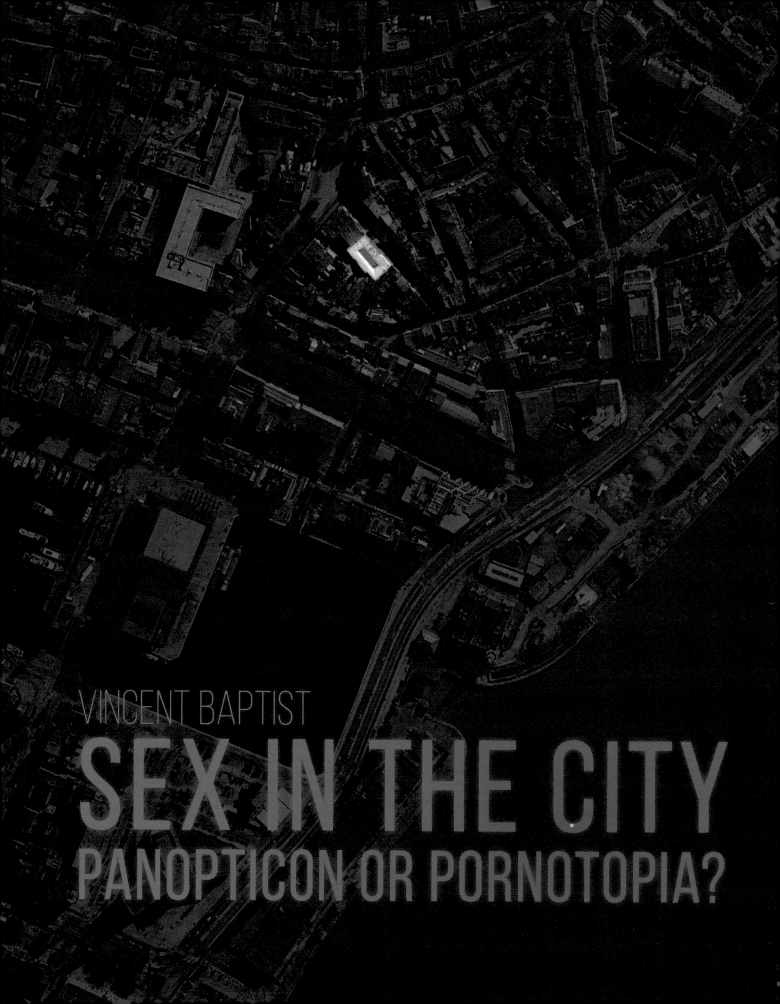

VINCENT BAPTIST

SEX IN THE CITY
PANOPTICON OR PORNOTOPIA?

Vincent Baptist is a lecturer and researcher at the School of History, Culture, and Communication at Erasmus University Rotterdam. He conducted his PhD research as part of the collaborative European research project "Pleasurescapes: Port Cities' Transnational Forces of Integration" and is affiliated with the Leiden-Delft-Erasmus research program PortCityFutures. He holds a research masters in media studies and has previously worked in the digital humanities research program CREATE (University of Amsterdam).

+ URBAN STUDIES, ARCHITECTURE, GENDER STUDIES

When paying a visit to Antwerp, Belgium's main port city, chances are that you will be nudged into visiting the Museum aan de Stroom (MAS). Opened in 2011 as Antwerp's largest museum, it houses a wide-ranging collection and exhibitions focused on the city, its residents and global historical connections created through maritime trade activities. While not nearly as eccentric or spectacular as Frank Gehry's Guggenheim Museum, the construction of the MAS clearly tried to surf the waves of the now ubiquitous "Bilbao effect." On the outside, the building's geometric alternation of glass and red sandstone elegantly guides the gaze of onlookers up to the MAS's freely accessible rooftop, where tourists can indulge in a panoramic view of the urban industrial surroundings. More surprising than the design and appeal of this new hotspot, however, is the fact that within walking distance of the MAS, another building can be found that epitomizes the nature of the modern port city, albeit according to a wholly different visual logic and character. In the adjacent Schipperskwartier (Skipper's Quarter) lies Villa Tinto, a former harbor warehouse turned mega brothel that concentrates virtually all of the city's sex work industry in one location.

Dubbed a "house of pleasure" on its central sign board, Villa Tinto appears as no less of an icon to the city of Antwerp than the MAS. As prostitution forms an almost inevitable part of the general public's shared imagination of urban maritime pasts, Villa Tinto embodies and exhibits the quintessential spirit of its host city as much as the MAS does. It also taps into the successful yet predictable formula of repurposing disused industrial infrastructure within contemporary urban landscapes. Villa Tinto encapsulates its surrounding port city environment, but the building's singularity also reaches beyond this specific context. In acting as an overarching hub for sex work in the city, it provides fruitful leads to reflect on how landscapes and infrastructures of sex—an inevitable but traditionally shunned part of the urban fabric—should function and appear. In addition, it constitutes a blueprint related to failed efforts and ongoing attempts to concentrate and centralize prostitution and sex work within urban environments. While the Bilbao Guggenheim has been translated into a kind of magic recipe that elevates cultural consumption in cities to unprecedented levels of iconicity, this essay discusses how (re)organizations of erotic consumption and corporeal beauty in contemporary cities have proven trickier to conceive and realize.

In order to explore the question of how infrastructures of sex work have been and could be integrated into–or isolated from–the built fabric of cities, this essay touches on several cases from Western Europe, specifically Belgium and the Netherlands. Prostitution regulation and legalization have arguably been developed and accepted more widely here than in many other parts of the world, congruent with the idea that "the urban geography of the sex industry and how visible it is varies from place to place in parallel with established moral standards."[1] Yet, a delicate point of discussion that has kept resurfacing on municipal policy agendas in the region over the past decades is the potential control, containment, or grouping together of sex work in such ways that limit their spread and potential nuisance within cities. Gianni Cito, who leads the Amsterdam-based architecture agency MOKE, which recently created a conceptual design for a new, all-encompassing "erotic center" to potentially replace the Dutch capital's notorious red-light district,[2] believes the issue of physically consolidating sex work is often pushed by defensive ideas and motives.[3] Municipal councilors seem mostly concerned with where to relocate all activities, rather than pondering the question of how a decisive solution should be designed and organized, particularly as a functional and safe space for workers and patrons alike. How should an environment of sex work look and feel?

Regardless of accompanying policy discussions and legislative changes, proposed ideals of centralized prostitution infrastructure act as clear signals of how sex work remains stigmatized and is allowed less leeway than other industries, even in seemingly open-minded urban environments. How, then, does one design a space for practices that are still deemed inappropriate, marginal, vulgar, or even immoral by certain groups and authorities in society? Should new kinds of erotic institutions be established with the actual aim to push away prostitution from everyday life? Or, in contrast, could architecture and planning help to further normalize sex in the city through the creation of publicly acknowledged and purpose-built zones?

The contemporary redevelopment of post-industrial sites and cities has increasingly trended toward commodification and sanitization – as exemplified by the phenomenon of the "Smooth City," whereby interrelated processes of gentrification, beautification, and commercialization reshape urban areas into seemingly perfect and frictionless leisure environments.[4] These trends also follow with respect to the development of spatial accommodations for sex work. An unrealized design concept from the late 1990s for a new, overarching red-light zone in the Dutch city of The Hague already anticipated this by imagining window prostitution along slick passageways with glass-walled container apartments on the sides, locking up sex workers into elusive but standardized work units.[5]

During the realization of Antwerp's Villa Tinto, which opened its doors in 2005, safety was touted as the overarching principle guiding the design process. At the same time, however, the project also aspired to deliver a site whose aesthetics would enhance the overall experience for both sex workers and their clientele. The well-known Belgian artist Arne Quinze was commissioned to help design the building and its facilities, after previously having expressed his personal interest in giving the sex trade business a more commendable style and beautiful appeal.[6] Quinze had previously established a label for design furniture characterized by bright colors and lean geometric shapes, and it is easy to imagine how such quirky aesthetics have stimulated Villa Tinto's lead partners to create "something 'trendy and unique' but also 'hygienic, ergonomic, and safe.'"[7]

This overall playful character may well invoke flirty Playboy-esque visions, but in this respect, it is worth pointing out that the once-ubiquitous erotic media and lifestyle empire was itself founded on hyper-masculine ideals. Praising modern architects and designers as the powerful urban bachelors that would create and inhabit exquisite penthouse apartments,[8] Playboy-branded spaces showcased masculine style and sophistication to such an extent that women were objectified alongside the tasteful furniture pieces. Playing into such tropes in the context of new sex work environments can thus potentially jeopardize and oppress female presence and agency. In addition, the so-called "pornotopic" infrastructures constituting the classic Playboy universe have always facilitated male comfort and seduction, often through high-tech innovations and gadgets.[9] However, the devices integrated into Villa Tinto's interiors are not technologies of pleasure. Rather, from multiple alarm buttons in every room to a fingerprint reader for employees, they clearly indicate that safety remains a key concern for sex workers, as they face threats of violence and exploitation seemingly endemic to the sex industry.

Despite their utopian aspirations and appeal, large-scale erotic centers and entertainment districts are not necessarily able to

provide an environment where everything harmlessly revolves around sexual beauty and bodily desire, even when tightly controlled and organized. Nicole Kalms attributes their potential risks and harm to the heterosexual dominance, male privilege, and gender-based objectification that remains ingrained in many urban sex landscapes.[10] Among others, Kalms points to the fact that many women often refrain from passing through sex-business zones in cities out of unease and fear of harassment. It makes me recall my own experience walking around the Villa Tinto block, together with my mother and sister. While spontaneously initiated out of fun and curiosity, the walk grew increasingly grim and uncomfortable as we tried to make our way through the sheer endless stream of male individuals and groups casting aggressively yearning looks, not only at Villa Tinto's show windows but also at any passersby who did not fit into the mono-masculine composition of the clientele swarming around outside the brothel walls. Villa Tinto's initiators may have put care in striking the right balance

between sexy and safe for the building's looks and interiors, but the adjacent public space makes for a less pretty picture.

According to Gianni Cito, the dynamic between interior and exterior space was one of the most important aspects in MOKE's concept for Amsterdam's new concentrated erotic center. Unlike Villa Tinto's direct surroundings, which remain sparsely developed, the famous De Wallen red-light district in Amsterdam's inner city boasts a large number of tourist-oriented facilities, which have only added to the area's popularity in recent times, as well as to its congestion. Overtourism in Amsterdam has caused an increasingly unmanageable and rowdy mass of visitors to be channeled through the narrow historical streets of De Wallen on a daily basis. Plans for redevelopment of the red-light district that were launched over the past decades in significant part stem from local policy makers' heightened sensitivity to the stereotypically "trashy" tourist that De Wallen primarily attracts, as well as to how these guests' local spending sustains criminogenic businesses in the neighborhood.[11] At MOKE, Cito sought to recapture the normal workings of an inner-city district: the resulting design aims to make casual wandering the focal activity again, no longer through blatantly commercialized and motel corridor-like streets, but along an upwardly spiraling trajectory where sex workers can present themselves. At the same time, workspaces of colleagues do not directly face each other anymore but rather look out over the captivating urban skyline.

With its curvy shapes and color palette that accentuate but do not overindulge in erotic spectacle, the MOKE design appears more sensible than both flashier and starker plans that stirred earlier debates in the Netherlands. During the 1970s, for instance, Rotterdam was under the spell of fierce protests against prostitution and accompanying criminal activities that had overrun Katendrecht, a disadvantaged neighborhood on the southern riverbanks of the port city. The municipal council tried to curb the social unrest and took stock of best practices in some German cities: new "eros flats" had been constructed there at the time, but the idea of erecting a dreary apartment building to function as a panopticon was mocked and challenged by Rotterdam residents.[12] By the late 1970s, Dutch architect Carel Weeber put a completely opposite plan on the table. One newspaper columnist wondered at the time: "Only the office building of a toaster company should look like a toaster. How would an eros center look?"[13] Perhaps like a giant penis? Weeber's solution for Katendrecht's troubles envisioned exactly that: a horizontal phallic building that would connect different pleasure facilities with one another.[14] The provocative idea was never realized, but it did place Weeber in a curious tradition of phallus-shaped building and landscape plans previously started by 18th-century French architects like Claude-Nicolas Ledoux and Pierre-Adrien Pâris.[15]

Weeber himself continued to muse about mass erotic infrastructures during later years, embracing the kitschiness that such designs could freely bring to overregulated built environments.[16] Granted, a penis-shaped brothel may be regarded as ecstatic and enticing in its overt materialization of sexuality,[17] but it is also still easy to dismiss as ugly and shallow. Henri Lefebvre once cried out "No, no!" when seeing plans for a "center for sexual relaxation" that mimicked female body parts, but produced little more than a sterile "pleasure machine" in his eyes.[18] The more contrived a brothel's appearance, then,

1 Magdalena Sabat, "Spatial Regulation of the Sex Industry in New York City," *LA+ Interdisciplinary Journal of Landscape Architecture* 2 (2015): 67, referencing Phil Hubbard & Teela Sanders, "Making Space for Sex Work: Female Street Prostitution and the Production of Urban Space," *International Journal of Urban and Regional Research* 27, no. 1 (2003): 75–89.

2 See Moke Architecten, "Erotisch Centrum," https://www.mokearchitecten.nl/portfolio/erotisch-centrum/ (accessed July 19, 2022).

3 All statements and opinions from Gianni Cito throughout the text have been obtained during a personal interview, conducted on June 21, 2022.

4 René Boer, "Smooth City is the New Urban," *Volume* 52 (2018), http://archis.org/volume/smooth-city-is-the-new-urban/.

5 Juliette Bekkering, "Red Light Zone," in Hans Ibelings (ed.), *The Artificial Landscape: Contemporary Architecture, Urbanism, and Landscape Architecture in the Netherlands* (NAi Publishers, 2000), 57.

6 Elaine Knutt, "Villa Tinto," *ICON* (March 23, 2007), https://www.iconeye.com/icon-026-august-2005/villa-tinto-icon-026-august-2005.

7 Annalee Newitz, "Hooking Up the Hookers," *WIRED* (November 1, 2005), https://www.wired.com/2005/11/hooking-up-the-hookers/.

8 See Playboy, "Playboy's Penthouse Apartment," in Joel Sanders (ed.), *Stud: Architectures of Masculinity* (Princeton Architectural Press, 1996), 54–67; and Beatriz Colomina, "Radical Interiority: Playboy Architecture 1953–1979," *Volume* 33 (2015), https://archis.org/volume/volume-33-beatriz-colomina-radical-interiority-playboy-architecture-1953-1979/.

9 Colomina, "Radical Interiority." For a further elaboration of this topic, see also Paul Preciado, *Pornotopia: An Essay on Playboy's Architecture and Biopolitics* (Zone Books, 2019).

10 Nicole Kalms, "No Harm Done? 'Sexual Entertainment Districts' Make the City a More Threatening Place for Women," *The Conversation* (August 9, 2017), https://theconversation.com/no-harm-done-sexual-entertainment-districts-make-the-city-a-more-threatening-place-for-women-81091. A further elaboration of this topic and argument can be found in Nicole Kalms, *Hypersexual City: The Provocation of Soft-Core Urbanism* (Routledge, 2017).

11 Manuel Aalbers, "Amsterdam," in Tsaiher Cheng (ed.), *Red Light City* (The Architecture Observer, 2016), 85–88.

Typical Red Light District street configuration, from straight to circular

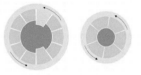

Enclosed private living rooms for sex workers, with work rooms around central social space

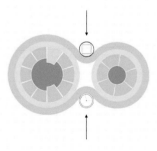

Network of strolling paths

Vertical circulation for elevators and fire exits

Hotel Rooms

Living Room

Office

Public Facilities

Street

the more it risks draining the very essence of what it tries to sell. In the meantime, however, newly envisioned erotic centers need to sell much more than just sex. The Belgian coastal town of Ostend is currently redeveloping a derelict port hangar into a mega brothel that will also house office spaces and a micro-brewery.[19] A more traditional idea of installing a new maritime museum in the old building was abandoned during earlier discussions. The Bilbao effect is surpassed by the Villa Tinto prototype.

MOKE's design also aims to offer a more holistic pleasure package. Capturing the breadth and scope of sex services, beyond merely prostitution, and other urban amusements within one building is what makes the project challenging and exciting, Gianni Cito says: "It would be too easy to come up with architectural concepts that are too simple, like a prison or a shopping mall." And again, there is the question of where in the city the erotic center would land, if approved by the municipal council. Cito points out Amsterdam's business district and financial hub, the Zuidas. Another male-dominated urban playground? Yes, "but our research showed that many internationals working there do make up an important part of the red-light district's clientele," Cito explains, "so why not bring De Wallen to its customers?" Among the corporate skyscrapers, a space could be carved out for a new, more sensual type of tower, one that may not necessarily reconcile all public opinions but at least stands tall and in harmony with the nature of a contemporary city.

Despite the growing predictability regarding "urban icons,"[20] a new eye-catching high-rise may well be an appropriate way forward to elevate the current visibility and status of sex work in cities, especially if a more inclusive scale of erotic desires and offerings can be safely accommodated in the process. Ascending the spiral hallway of MOKE's proposed erotic center would then be not too far removed from walking up the MAS's public staircase, with the difference that visitors are not chasing the ultimate rooftop selfie but instead surrendering to perpetual circling, glancing, and seductive *flânerie*. After all, is that not what has made modern cities beautiful and appealing in the first place?

12 Vincent Baptist & Paul van de Laar, "Pleasure Reconsidered and Relocated: Modern Urban Visions in the Wake of Rotterdam's Discontinued Amusement Areas," in Carola Hein, Robert Bartłomiejski & Maciej Kowalewski (eds), *Hustle and Bustle: The Vibrant Cultures of Port Cities* (Brill, forthcoming).

13 Hans Kok, "In de stad," *NRC Handelsblad* (January 4, 1979), 8.

14 Baptist & Van de Laar, "Pleasure Reconsidered and Relocated" (forthcoming).

15 Adélaïde de Caters, "Instituciones de libertinaje," in Adélaïde de Caters & Rosa Ferré (eds), *1000 m2 de deseo: Arquitectura y sexualidad* (Centro de Cultura Contemporánea de Barcelona, 2016), 29–32; Adélaïde de Caters, "El espacio como trampa," in Adélaïde de Caters & Rosa Ferré (eds), *1000 m2 de deseo: Arquitectura y sexualidad* (Centro de Cultura Contemporánea de Barcelona, 2016), 65.

16 Rik Kuiper, "Welke ideale stad moet in het Markermeer verrijzen? Schetsen van Utopia," *Quest* (May, 2007), 24–25.

17 For an essay that more thoroughly reflects on the bonds between ecstasy, erotics and architecture, see Neil Leach "Ecstasy," in Charles Jencks (ed.), *Ecstatic Architecture: The Surprising Link* (Academy Editions, 1999), 66–77.

18 Henri Lefebvre, *Toward an Architecture of Enjoyment* (University of Minnesota Press, 2014), 48.

19 Alan Hope, "Coming Soon to Ostend: Mega-Brothel with Own Police Station," *The Brussels Times* (August 4, 2021), https://www.brusselstimes.com/news/belgium-all-news/180094/coming-soon-to-ostend-mega-brothel-with-own-police-station.

20 See Maria Kaika, "Autistic Architecture: The Fall of the Icon and the Rise of the Serial Object of Architecture," *Environment and Planning D: Society and Space* 29, no. 6 (2011): 968–92.

Previous: Model of Carel Weeber's design for the Katendrecht eros center.

Opposite: Program organization diagrams of MOKE's proposed erotic center in Amsterdam.

ADRIAN BEJAN

THE PHYSICS OF BEAUTY

Adrian Bejan is the J.A. Jones Distinguished Professor of Mechanical Engineering at Duke University. He is ranked among the top 0.01% of the most cited and impactful world scientists and has authored 30 books, including *Time and Beauty* (2022). He was the recipient of the 2018 Benjamin Franklin Medal for his pioneering interdisciplinary contributions in thermodynamics and constructal theory.

✚ PHYSICS, CONSTRUCTAL THEORY

What is beauty, and what is lack of beauty? Why do we seek beautiful objects, settings, and images in front of us and in our minds? For early humans in prehistoric times, before there was the word "beauty," there was undoubtedly the feeling, the perception, and the understanding of it. In the broadest, simplest sense of the term, beauty is the descriptor for the human feeling of attractiveness. This leads us to describe things as diverse as paintings hanging in galleries, calligraphy, fashion, music, dance, gesture (courtesy), mathematical proofs, and even a winning shot in tennis as beautiful. The definition also holds for the opposite of beauty: ugliness is the word for repulsiveness – the feeling of disgust and human desire to retreat from what was perceived. That questions of beauty–or ugliness, for that matter–persist is proof that to define beauty in scientific terms is not easy. Why is beauty so important? While there are many places to turn for answers, physics can offer some impartial insight.

The physics that underpins the impression of beauty is in how people perceive their immediate environment, their "niche." It is general, measurable, and impersonal – the facts, like in all physics. The easiest introduction to the physics of beauty is to start with visual perception. Our eyes scan the environment in abrupt, fast, and high frequency jolts called saccades. What is transmitted from the retina to the brain is the change, which is the surprise in the new image that has just taken shape. Change after change is the perception of time, the feeling that time passes, and that time passes faster as we get older.[1]

It occurred to me that most of the famous paintings hanging in galleries around the world are rectangularly shaped like a business card or paragraphs on a page. This coincidence can be explained using physics: such shapes are able to be scanned faster – a useful quality. The wall has a finite area and the time that the viewer has is finite as well. So, scanning (movement) on an area is physics, and to sweep an area faster and faster by morphing the shape of the area is evolution, evolutionary design, or what I refer to as "constructal design."[2]

As most animals–including humans–move through the environment, their eyes are scanning the field of vision, which is elongated, looking like a rectangle. It is two-dimensional, defined by a vertical dimension H, and horizontal dimension L. The long dimension is aligned with the horizontal because the field of vision is about our world, which looks flat in the distance. The two eyes of common animals are aligned with the world, horizontally. Utilizing physics, we can therefore determine the area that is scanned the fastest has a shape with an aspect ratio L/H approximately equal to 3/2, which correlates to the ubiquitous (or "access") shape of the business card, credit card, cinema screen, computer screen, painting, banknote, airline ticket, flags of nations, and, as had occurred to me, most of the famous paintings hanging in galleries around the world.

This so-called access shape is ubiquitous because it serves a purpose, which has a physical basis: grasping the image faster is beneficial to animal life.[3] Fast perception is essential for avoiding danger and finding food, a mate, and shelter. This holds true for all the animals endowed with vision – runners, swimmers, and fliers. This is also why our "human and machine" species[4] has evolved from lighthouses, sirens, and headlights to radar, night vision, and GPS: fast perception of danger helps us survive. Our evolution as a species is essentially geared toward a design of how to move faster and more economically, more safely, and for longer duration through the environment, leading to a longer lifetime in the landscape.

The theory behind the ubiquity of the access shape also accounts for the shapes of objects that from classical antiquity to our era have been attributed to God. The "divine proportion" (or golden ratio) is an irrational number (1.618). Unlike the L/H shapes of the objects mentioned above, the divine proportion cannot be the result of measuring an observed object: the exact number 1.618 agrees with the theoretical 3/2, which is an order of magnitude. This reveals that the reason the golden ratio has been associated with beautiful objects is that their images are grasped faster. The difference is that to observe a shape and call it divine proportion is description, empiricism: observe first and describe later. To predict that an object shaped this way will convey the feeling of beauty is theory, which means seeing with the eyes of the mind, and comparing with observations later.

This physical basis of beauty therefore unveils the mechanism of human perception, which is like a game of Tetris in which a successful move takes place when a new block falls into a waiting gap so that the wall of blocks becomes bigger and stronger. How the Tetris player rotates the new block to make it fit in the waiting gap is an individual act that belongs to the player. How the block was oriented to fit is not necessarily how it was oriented before it arrived. That is why perception is personal, belonging to the individual. But why does the mind try to make sense of a new input – to play this game of Tetris? Why is there a natural tendency to organize the fresh input to make it fit among past receptions? The answer that comes from physics is one, and it is general: it is to empower the individual with speed and clarity of thought, understanding, decision-making, and physical movement (life) on the earth's surface.

A beautiful image is, however, more than just the L/H shape that is everywhere. There are plenty of ugly business cards floating around the world – their shape only determines the speed by which we can scan, and therefore perceive them as distinct within the environment. Beauty is in the *balance* conveyed by the image. Balance is a more general way of looking at the physics basis of beauty: the balance in the scanning effort translates into ease of understanding and public dissemination of the idea.

Beautiful images of nature have several additional features that convey balance in three main ways. First, the observed shapes are surprisingly few. One is the profile of the cone, pyramid, or pyre to light a fire. The height is comparable with the base, but smaller. Each shape comes in many sizes, and the larger are few and the smaller are many. Another shape is that of birds and airplanes. It is perceived as a self-standing shape because the wingspan is essentially the same as the body length. This shape is predicted based on the constructal law[5] and it comes with a hierarchical distribution of sizes, few large and many small. Hierarchy, harmony, and stasis convey balance. Together they represent the physical basis of *diversity*, which is why diversity happens naturally and has staying power.

Second, a beautiful, balanced image has contrast, sharp lines, or different colors and shades. We take contrast for granted. Why? Because when absent, the contrast is enhanced by scanning. Look at the top row in Figure 1. The transition from one shade to the next appears sharp. It looks sharper than it should because every shade of gray is uniform, as you can see in the bottom row. In the top row, in the vicinity of the transition the change is accentuated by the scanning process. The scanning transmits (and the brain records) the change, not the lack of change. So, with the tendency to accentuate contrast comes the phenomenon of illusion, which is useful in this case and in the profession of magicians.

You get the same impression when you scan Figure 2 vertically, from bottom to top. Which rectangle is taller? The upper rectangle seems slightly taller because we perceive more changes as we scan it vertically, but that is not the impression you get from the lower rectangle when you scan it in the same way. In fact, this is an illusion and the two "rectangles" are actually the same square. If you rotate Figure 2 by 90 degrees, you have the feeling that the other is taller.

Finally, the beautiful image has perspective, which is the depth of the image. Perspective is the name for the virtual third dimension of the two-dimensional field of vision. Imagine driving down a flat highway – the road and sky converges, conveying to the mind the third dimension of the image: perspective. Now, look at your surroundings and question what you see. There are no parallel lines in the human field of vision. This is contrary to the teachings we receive in geometry and the rest of the sciences, where we use rulers to make parallel lines. We can see the difference between beauty and lack of beauty when we look at drawings of "nature" published in scientific journals: a drawing with parallel lines does not look good. The beautiful

Figure 1

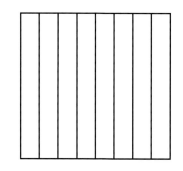

Figure 2

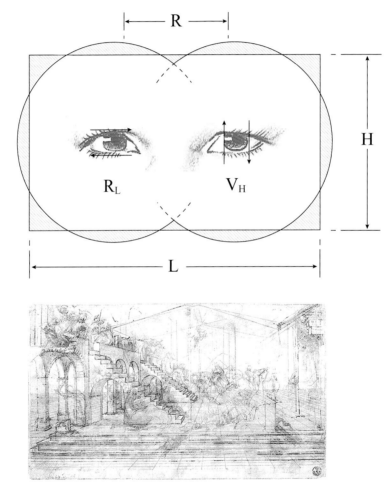

drawing is the one with lines that converge to virtual points on the line of the horizon, the representational technique that we owe to Filippo Brunelleschi.

Beyond scanning the environment with our eyes to perceive beautiful images, the connection between facile movement and attractive feeling is familiar if we think of "scanning" an area with our feet. Inhabited areas acquire their shape naturally from the urge of every individual to have access to the whole territory – "desire" lines in landscapes emerge for a reason. We scan the earth with our feet, vehicles, and communications, and it is this movement that constitutes social organization. There are many directions, many movers, and immense freedom to change things and ways. This, the freedom to change everything that affects our movement in life is the physical basis of creativity, the act of creating ideas, artifacts, and decisions.

The physics of beauty highlights the importance of questioning what we perceive, what we see, what we hear, and what we read. Questioning is what opens the eyes of the young to what is really going on. Coincidences that come from observing and questioning are extremely important. Every "a-ha!" we hear on the path from coincidences to connections is like a Gordian knot that gets cut in one blow, with a heavy axe. Coincidences happen, like the agreement between the falling block and the gap that awaits it in the Tetris game. Once inside the gap, the block and the wall are the new connection. The wall has several waiting gaps because its many bricks are the earlier connections, from earlier coincidences that screamed for a principle. The new principle is the new physics.

The physics of perception is an important step for science because previously beauty was categorized as intangible, out-of-reach, and not belonging in physics. In fact, beauty belongs in physics along with other intangibles due to human perception and cognition: the urge to have freedom, to organize, to have wealth, to live with others. Vision, cognition, and locomotion are features of a single design for movement of animal mass with easier access in time, all over the globe. Balance is everywhere in nature, notably in the harmony between few large and many small, and few fast and many slow.

1 Adrian Bejan, *Time and Beauty: Why Time Flies and Beauty Never Dies* [World Scientific, 2022].

2 Adrian Bejan & J. Peder Zane, *Design in Nature: How the Constructal Law Governs Evolution in Biology, Physics, Technology, and Social Organization* [Doubleday, 2012]; Adrian Bejan, *The Physics of Life: The Evolution of Everything* [St. Martin's Press, 2016].

3 Bejan, *The Physics of Life*.

4 Adrian Bejan, "Human Evolution is Biological and Technological Evolution," *BioSystems* 195 [2020]: 104156; Adrian Bejan, *Shape and Structure, From Engineering to Nature* [Cambridge University Press, 2000].

5 Adrian Bejan, *Freedom and Evolution: Hierarchy in Nature, Society and Science* [Springer Nature, 2020].

VISCERAL

JEFFREY BLANKENSHIP + JESSICA HAYES-CONROY

"The older I grow and the longer I look at landscapes and seek to understand them, the more convinced I am that their beauty is not simply an aspect but their very essence, and that that beauty derives from the human presence. For far too long we have told ourselves that the beauty of a landscape was the expression of some transcendent law: the conformity to certain universal esthetic principles or the conformity to certain biological or ecological laws...The beauty that we see in the vernacular landscape is the image of our common humanity: hard work, stubborn hope, and mutual forbearance striving to be love. I believe that a landscape which makes these qualities manifest is one that can be called beautiful."[1]

J.B. Jackson

Jeffrey Blankenship is an associate professor of architectural studies at Hobart and William Smith Colleges in Geneva, NY, where he teaches the history of modern landscape architecture and design studios. He is currently working on a monograph for the LSU Press, *Everyday Modernity: J. B. Jackson and Landscape Magazine, 1951–1968*.

Jessica Hayes-Conroy is an associate professor of women's studies at Hobart and William Colleges in Geneva, NY, where she teaches critical perspectives on health and the body. Her work within the field of visceral geography uses feminist corporeal scholarship to theorize the body as a relational and developmental emergence.

+ HISTORY, AESTHETICS, VISCERAL GEOGRAPHY

Although the 20th-century essayist John Brinckerhoff Jackson (1909–1996) never offered a definitive statement on beauty or its qualities, it was a topic that made frequent appearances in his writing as an often inflexible and limited aesthetic ideal that, nevertheless, had the potential to be redefined as a more inclusive concept. In the aggregate, Jackson's body of work on landscape reveals a philosophy of beauty that we believe is worth examining and building upon as a basis for contemporary praxis. As the passage on the previous page suggests, Jackson's understanding of beauty privileged the emergent qualities of lived experience over static philosophical prescriptions or appeals to a natural archetype. Beauty was not something that could be pre-determined for Jackson; rather, beauty was practiced in the living out of daily life. In this sense, the felt qualities of what we will later call *visceral beauty* supplanted the visual in Jackson's work, signaling a shrewd attention to the living, working, and sensing human body. Indeed, at times the body itself seems to form the very basis for his unique conception of beauty. The body was his compass for understanding what was missing from conventional definitions of beauty, and often also for defending what was scorned by those same definitions. To be sure, Jackson's interest in the embodied, lived landscape stretched beyond musings on beauty; still, we find his attempts to articulate beauty especially instructive for understanding his approach to landscape more broadly. These occasional musings on beauty help to reveal what he saw, or felt, in the landscape. They are also, we will argue, part of what establishes his contemporary relevance, especially in regard to matters of sustainability.

In a collection of essays spanning 45 years, J. B. Jackson developed a critical perspective on the American landscape that continues to be influential in landscape architecture and many other disciplines today. As the editor of the interdisciplinary magazine *Landscape* from 1951 to 1968, and a public intellectual, his frequently featured essays commented on any subject he believed would inform a more nuanced understanding of the forces that were transforming the mid-20th-century American landscape. Jackson's earliest essays in the magazine used the term landscape in a way that was not common outside of the field of human geography. Here, landscape didn't describe a picturesque or painterly scene, a process of beautification, or a wilderness ideal. Instead, Jackson wrote of landscapes that seemed somewhat prosaic: the everyday, ordinary environments of small cities and towns, mechanized farms, mobile dwellings, highways, and the commercial strip. This humanistic approach to studying the everyday environment struck a chord with some mid-century scholars, designers, and planners who were drawn to Jackson's questioning of the aesthetic orthodoxies that dominated the landscape discourses of the 1950s, 1960s, and beyond.

To understand Jackson's ideas around beauty and appreciate their contemporary relevance, we first need to establish what he found wanting in the rhetoric of his time. J. B. Jackson operated as a frequent antagonist to the mid-20th-century environmental design professions most concerned with shaping the built and natural environment – landscape architecture, architecture, and planning. The common language shared by these disciplines had become as abstract as the formal geometries and unadorned masses of modern buildings and the "objective" layers of Ian McHarg's landscape analysis. *Space* had replaced scenery, *form* had replaced ornament and symbol, *function* had replaced style, *health* had replaced meaning, *man* and *society* had replaced local community, and *nature* was something to view through the plate-glass window, or, soon enough, Landsat imagery. At the center of Jackson's critical reaction to the aesthetic, social, and environmental agendas of these disciplines was a fundamental sympathy for the often-messy lived experiences that unfolded in the American landscape – experiences that were rarely accommodated within the rigidly dogmatic

frameworks of modernist design or environmental planning. In Jackson's essays, book reviews, and editorials he paints the design and planning professions as disconnected in their devotion to abstract principles, and as unconcerned with these lived realities.

While the adherents of modernist design and planning found beauty in new technologies and methods, and the potential for a totally planned environment, Jackson sought beauty in more everyday modernities – the social, economic, technological, and ecological realities of life in the 20th century that were impacting even the most remote landscapes and their inhabitants. As the quotation that opens this essay suggests, Jackson had little use for concepts of beauty that emerged from either universal compositional principles or from appeals to nature as the fundamental (biological/ecological/evolutionary) source of all aesthetic "laws." Instead, beauty for Jackson was a result of human life embedding itself into the land. However, in Jackson's writings throughout his career, the landscape was not just a passive visual artifact of these human processes, nor was his an intellectualized insistence that we should somehow learn to appreciate the mundane and banal out of a sense of egalitarian solidarity with the "common man." Rather, for Jackson there was always a reciprocal relationship between the physical landscape and human experience that did not presuppose any visual or intellectual definition of beauty. Beauty, for Jackson, could not exist outside the network of human and nonhuman relationships that emerge in the course of everyday life; it could not be reduced to a one-way sensory experience.

In rebuffing arguments for beauty as a definable quality emerging from universally held visual preferences or from "natural" laws, Jackson was more pointedly rejecting all prescriptive aesthetic dictates and instead proposing something much more *avant garde*–arguably even political–in its implications for why beauty matters. In his essay "To Pity the Plumage and Forget the Dying Bird," Jackson addressed the impacts of poverty on

the American landscape.[2] He argued (as the title suggests) that critics paid too much attention to the surface aesthetics of outwardly degraded landscapes while failing to inquire about the basic conditions needed for sustaining human life. Rebuking this failure, Jackson argued, "the moment we get the courage to blame poverty for some of our environmental troubles, we will have taken the first step to reform." He specifically calls out the "Beautificationists" in this essay for ignoring the economic explanation for these "deliberate affronts to the passerby," explaining that "by this time everyone ought to know that junked cars in a farmyard or a pasture...mean poverty."[4] Later in the essay, Jackson more directly discusses beauty as a matter of collective responsibility.

> It would be encouraging to believe that the environmental designers, particularly the landscape architects, could in time direct this war against poverty. ...But what is also essential is for every responsible American to add a new social dimension to his definition of landscape beauty. We will have to see that an inhabited landscape is neither beautiful nor sound unless it makes possible the unfolding of the individual in work and social relationships as much as in health and recreation.[5]

It's important to note that such overtly political statements as Jackson offered in "To Pity the Plumage"–going so far as to suggest a "guaranteed annual income"[6]–were rare in his writing. In fact, Jackson's work has been critiqued for failing to engage with the role of "income and wealth inequities, racial/gender/religious discrimination, and environmental degradation" in the production of the American landscapes that he so often optimistically celebrated.[7] While this may be true in much of Jackson's writing, we are also compelled by the way that he sharply attends to bodily needs and desires in both this and other essays–to the "habits" of poverty, for example–that start to connect the individual to the structural in politically important ways. His insistence in addressing poverty is not abstract and theoretical but deeply intimate; those who overlook poverty are forgetting about real people and their need to get on with the unfolding of life, perhaps even (as we all deserve) in ways that allow for moments of pleasure in the midst of it all. This is a story line that, in some ways, runs through much of Jackson's writing. For Jackson, a landscape could not be beautiful if it didn't sustain and propel human life. But, even in the so-called "ugly," resource-poor, impoverished landscapes that others criticized, Jackson always seemed to find (some) beauty in the human will to survive.

This sensibility about the body appears in various places throughout Jackson's work. Beginning in the earliest issues of *Landscape* magazine, Jackson took on the modern movement in architecture, and its manifestations in landscape architecture and planning. While finding much to admire in the expressive forms and social conscience of modernist design and planning, he also found the proposals of many designers and planners "as intolerant of the individual's undisciplined aspirations as of the undisciplined forces of nature."[8] In other words, what the designers and planners lacked wasn't a certain aesthetic sensibility but an appreciation for the chaotic unfolding of human and nonhuman life – for the habits and happenstances of daily lived experience that could not be so neatly accounted. Today, of course, climate change has taught the design professions a great deal about the hubris of discounting "nature's" undisciplined forces, but perhaps we need a similar reckoning regarding those "less rational aspects of the individual" as well.[9] Indeed, these two are not mutually exclusive. Jackson consistently argued for nature to be considered as omnipresent in all landscapes and aspects of human life, seeing nature as deeply interconnected with our social, emotional, and perceptual experiences.

It is instructive, then, that Jackson spent much of his life defending the very landscapes that were scorned by people concerned with both scenic and environmental quality. Why did he do it? What did he see in these landscapes that others did not? Many establishment critics railed against the "visual blight" of the vast and expanding highway landscapes and roadside developments that were cropping up to accommodate the automobile's increasing dominance of American life. Jackson would not disagree that the highway strip is, in some sense, an environmental and aesthetic disaster: he himself called Route 66 hideous (a landscape we might now call charming). And yet he insisted on seeing such landscapes through the perspective of lived experience, as though this changed everything. Because it did. Jackson's approach to the highway strip signaled a deep attention to the getting-on of human life – to the sensations, cravings, moods, and desires that propelled the American landscape into motion. In "Other-Directed Houses" (1956), Jackson defends the visual clutter of the highway strip by suggesting a sense of viscerally felt relief from the long human absence and depravations of the open road:

> I keep remembering the times when I have driven for hour after hour across an emptiness–desert or prairie–which was *not* blemished by highway stands, and how relieved and delighted I always was to finally see somewhere in the distance the jumble of billboards and gas pumps and jerry-built houses. Tourist traps or not, these were very welcome sights, and even the commands to EAT, COME AS YOU ARE, GAS UP, GET FREE ICE WATER AND STICKERS, had a comforting effect...The gaudier the layout, the nicer it seemed, and its impact on the surrounding landscape bothered me not at all.[10]

Countering the mounting public indignation of the highway strip, Jackson seemed to be saying: do you not see how life unfolds within these spaces? How these spaces attend to the unfolding of life? In drawing attention to the highway strip as an embodied phenomenon, Jackson was privileging a certain "perceptual generosity"[11] that helped to underscore beauty as a more visceral phenomenon. Put another way, while the

critics practiced "the type of suspicion that grounds the act of judgement in a practice of critique,"[12] Jackson's conception of beauty began not with critique but with the practice of human life itself. His was perceptually generous because it was sympathetic to what the body needs to get on–a momentary sensation, an anticipated respite, a common pleasure–anything that carries one forward.

For Jackson, therefore, the body redeems the highway strip *as (at least somewhat) beautiful* because it is what the body needs at that moment – a place to roll in looking ratty as hell, have a cool drink, and give your complaining kids some stickers to play with. A sense of physical and visual relief after miles of undifferentiated countryside informs an emotional response that Jackson suggests manifests as "fleeting beauty."[13] Using the example of musical preferences, affect theorist Ben Anderson similarly describes this phenomenon as a momentary visceral connection to the world in which the only judgment made, the only expression of taste, is that it simply "feels right" in that moment.[14] This shift in attention from a universal, objective quality to a unique, embodied sensation fundamentally challenges any fixed or moralistic notion of scenic quality. This is what we want to point to as *visceral beauty* – a practice of judgment that is ephemeral, emergent, and elastic, but also, deeply tangible and impactful, attentive to the immediacy of embodied experience.

In his example of the highway strip, Jackson was careful to explain that even though he *liked* this piece of the American landscape, he was not dismissive of its "frequent depravity and confusion and dirt." "Its potentialities for trouble–esthetic, social and economic," he continued, were "as great as its potentialities for good." Jackson asks: "how are we to tame this force unless we understand it and even develop a kind of love for it?"[15] Retrospectively, "this force" seems to point to a whole lot more than the highway strip: the American love-affair with the automobile, cheap gasoline, the need for

speed, the rise of consumer capitalism and unregulated growth, convenience products and the embodied problems they solved, suburbanization and the (white, heterosexual) nuclear family, the way blacktop traps heat in the summer, etc. Jackson's work doesn't necessarily ignore all this but rather traverses a clear path through it, centering embodied experience in a way that seems both unsurprising and refreshing. What, then, if we read "this force" that Jackson was interested in knowing, loving, *and taming* as simply visceral beauty at large? That is, the things—objects, ideas, sensations, encounters, topographies—that the body is drawn to, the relational experiences that just "feel right," in moment after moment of life living itself out in particular places and times. While on the one hand, stickers and ice water might seem like some rather ridiculous reasons to defend these problematic landscapes and the structures that created them, what Jackson's work shows us more broadly is that it is imperative to always understand landscape as a relational and affective phenomenon in which the body plays a central role.

In 2015, the landscape architectural theorist Elizabeth Meyer argued that "aesthetic experience occurs within an affective world that implicates bodies, spaces, values, experiences, and networks." She continues, "A theory and practice of landscape affects and effects would recognize that encounters between people and places are exchanges of emotions, agency, and energies."[16] Drawing from contemporary theories of affect, Meyer's ideas of beauty seem to resonate strongly with Jackson's sensibilities in numerous ways. She calls for a landscape architecture inspired to consider "'the business of affections and aversions, of how the world strikes the body on its sensory surfaces, of that which takes root in the gaze and the guts and all that arises from our most banal, biological insertion into the world.'"[17] All of this seems to align with Jackson's description of beauty in the highway strip, and elsewhere. Beauty is alive in the mundane, the embodied moments of life – the multi-scalar intersections between self and world.

Meyer's project is a worthy one. She is concerned with sustainability, and particularly with how to harness the power of aesthetic experience toward the goal of building more sustainable and just ways of life. Setting aside some important critiques of the term sustainability (there's a lot about our current reality that we don't particularly want to sustain), we share this goal. Meyer explains her intent thusly,

> I believe that, as a body of knowledge and as a way of experiencing the world, social aesthetics can play a critical role in a sustainability agenda. It will take more than ecologically regenerative designs for our early twenty-first-century neoliberal consumer culture to be sustainable. What is needed are designed landscapes that provoke those who experience them to be more aware of how their actions affect the environment, and to care enough to make changes in their actions. This involves the recognition of the role of aesthetic environmental experiences, such as beauty, wonder, awe, ugliness, and repulsion, in re-centering human consciousness from an egocentric to a more biocentric perspective. Such a recognition is dependent on new conceptions of human and nonhuman entanglements.[18]

Perhaps this is one way to think about what it might mean to "tame" visceral beauty – a deliberate social aesthetic project that seeks to harness the affective body and retrain it toward more ecologically conscientious habits and affectations. But, we would also argue that we need to be careful with the assumption that the problem lies in how much people care, or in their level of awareness of environmental issues. These aren't generous assumptions, perceptually or otherwise. Moreover, as Jackson points to in "To Pity the Plumage," it would be a mistake not to recognize the structural forces at play in environmental catastrophe (after all, junked cars in the countryside are about a hell of a lot more than not caring). Drawing from Jackson's lessons, the body matters much more basically here: if we want to understand how to live more sustainably, we need to take the force of visceral beauty seriously; we need to recognize that much of the unfolding of life happens in and through these mundane practices of judgment. I need ice water. My kids need stickers. Marketing companies and advertisers seem to understand this all too well; what would happen if landscape architects and environmental planners did too?

To tame can mean to harness, master, or subdue; in this sense, it is probably not an appropriate metaphor for what we are getting at. But *taming* also has connotations of healing, caring for, and harmonious cohabitation. For us, the project of aesthetics and sustainability is less about convincing people to care as it is about recognizing the need for more people to be cared for; it is less about teaching people to be aware of environmental problems as it is about becoming aware of social ones. The getting-on of life will continue (until it doesn't), unsustainably or otherwise. If we want to encourage people to live more sustainably, we first have to understand how they live – how they cope, get by, make decisions, survive. It's telling that when Jackson spoke most directly about his ideas for reform, the solution was social, economic, and political – give people more to live on. To be perceptually generous in the moment of climate crisis, we must recognize that many of the unsustainable habits that drive us toward extinction are judgments that feel right in the moment. Why do we cling to these habits in the first place? What problems are they solving, and how could we otherwise solve them? This seems to be the most pressing task in front of us: to really lean into all the "junked cars" of today – Amazon boxes piling up on porches of gentrified neighborhoods, disposable coffee cups fueling 60-hour work weeks, depression meds to deal with the realities of crushing debt, the comforting distractions of cat videos on social media, energy bars replacing meals we don't have time to cook – and as we lean in, to really hear the stories that these embodied habits tell us about our (uneven) survival, and our (collective) demise.

1 John Brinckerhoff Jackson, *Discovering the Vernacular Landscape* (Yale University Press, 1984), xii.

2 J. B. Jackson, "To Pity the Plumage and Forget the Dying Bird," *Landscape* 17, no. 1 (1967): 1–4.

3 Ibid., 3.

4 Ibid.

5 Ibid., 4.

6 Ibid., 3.

7 Mitchell Schwarzer, "Selected Books by J. B. Jackson," *Harvard Design Magazine* (Fall 1998), http://www.harvarddesignmagazine.org/issues/6/selected-books-by-j-b-jackson.

8 J. B. Jackson, "Review of Garrett Eckbo," *Landscape for Living, Landscape* 2, no. 3 (1953): 34.

9 Ibid., 35.

10 J. B. Jackson, "Other-Directed Houses," *Landscape* 6, no. 2 (1956–1957): 29.

11 Ben Anderson, "Practices of Judgement and Domestic Geographies of Affect," *Social & Cultural Geography* 6, no. 5 (2005): 649.

12 Ibid.

13 Jackson, "Other-Directed Houses," 30.

14 Anderson, "Practices of Judgement," 646.

15 Jackson, "Other-Directed Houses," 30.

16 Elizabeth K. Meyer, "Beyond Sustaining Beauty: Musings on a Manifesto," in Elen Deming (ed.), *Values in Landscape Architecture and Environmental Design: Finding center in theory and practice* (LSU Press, 2015), 35.

17 Terry Eagleton quoted in Meyer, ibid., 36.

18 Ibid., 31–32.

DRAWING LANDSCAPE

SANDA ILIESCU

Sanda Iliescu teaches art and architecture at the University of Virginia. Educated as an architect, she is a practicing artist who has exhibited her paintings, drawings, and collages in the United States and Europe. She is the editor of *The Hand and the Soul: Aesthetics and Ethics in Architecture and Art* and the author of *Experiencing Art and Architecture: Lessons on Looking*. She has received numerous awards, among them the Rome Prize.

+ ART

Opposite: *Landscapes of Waste* (2009), created using leftover materials and detritus (graphite dust, pencil shavings, etc.) collected during the drawing process for *Poem Drawing*.

Is it still possible to create a meaningful picture of a landscape? Can an artist in our time of environmental crisis make a drawing or painting that is true to both nature's beauty and its desperate fragility?

The problem is not only that the beautiful drawings and paintings that have come down to us from the past may seem inadequate to us because they fail to address the kind of dangers that our natural world faces today, it is also that the very system of linear perspective that many of these works of art rely upon evokes a degree of human control and mastery over nature that we may now consider problematic. This sense of mastery comes from the perspectival system and the way it revolves around the creation of an implied ideal observer, one who dominates the land and indeed shapes it according to their will. Seen from the point of view of this observer, nature becomes an orderly construct, one structured around a single horizon, a finite number of vanishing points, and, very often, a tripartite division of space into foreground, middle ground, and background. In these pictures, the artist arrests the landscape and reduces it to an image seen in a single moment in time by a single observer at a particular location in space. Because the sense of time in this system is so fixed, there is no easy way to convey nature's continual transformation. Neither is there an easy way to evoke the complex multisensory experiences of a place – to highlight the richness of the sense of smell, hearing, touch, temperature, humidity, and air movements among other intertwined perceptions and sensations. Classical Western images of landscapes tend to deny this fluidity and project onto nature instead a sense of coherence and completeness – an absence of the element of change. Their beauty–their enchantment–has much to do with this sense of stillness and composure.

The story of modern art in the West–and of modern depictions of nature–is a story of the dismantling of the system of linear perspective, with its implications of closure, fixity, and privileged visuality. Through abstraction, performance art, earthworks, collaborative and participatory projects, and socially engaged work, modern and contemporary artists have created compelling alternatives to the traditional perspectival picture of nature.[1]

In my own landscape drawings, I seek to counter the perspectival system by exploring ideas of formal openness and incompleteness and, at times, by making and exhibiting works of art that are unfinished. Many of my nature drawings

Poem Drawing: A Little Less Returned for Him Each Spring, No. 1

Poem Drawing: A Little Less Returned for Him Each Spring, No. 2

Poem Drawing: A Little Less Returned for Him Each Spring, No. 13

Poem Drawing: A Little Less Returned for Him Each Spring, No. 14

Poem Drawing series [2002 to present] is created with graphite and colored pencil on paper, 12 in. x 20.5 in.

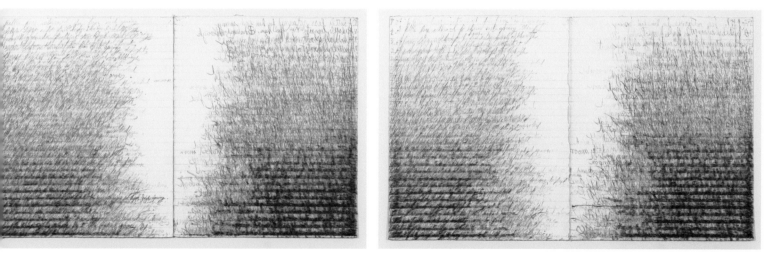

Poem Drawing: A Little Less Returned for Him Each Spring, No. 5

Poem Drawing: A Little Less Returned for Him Each Spring, No. 10

Poem Drawing: A Little Less Returned for Him Each Spring, No. 19

Poem Drawing: A Little Less Returned for Him Each Spring, No. 20

have been inspired by the work of German landscape architects Peter and Anneliese Latz and by their conception of the landscape as both open and unfinished. Peter Latz once told me that there was no such thing as a "finished" park or garden, and that there was no natural state that was ideal or desirable above all others.[2] Rather, in nature, everything was always in flux: trees grew and matured, plants thrived or died off, new species took hold, levels of toxicity changed, soils deposited and eroded. As a result, there was no such thing as a fixed landscape, but rather a series of intertwined, unfolding processes. For the Latzes, the discipline of landscape architecture thus resists the closure of the finished artifact more than painting, music, literature, or architecture. For them, the work of the landscape architect must include not only an initial set of explorations and interventions but also the subsequent study of the consequences of those first design acts, as well the obligation to continue to propose potential new actions. Initial conjectures and interventions, they argue, must be reevaluated and revised in a process that remains fundamentally open.

The series of drawings I began in 2002 titled *Poem Drawing: A Little Less Returned for Him Each Spring* is my attempt to bring the Latzes' open vision of landscape to a work of art. In them, I set out not so much to "draw" anything, but rather to enact a "drawing" process that, like a park or garden, unfolds over time and through a particular sequence of stages. The drawings take Wallace Stevens's poem *Anglaise Mort à Florence* as their point of departure, a poem in eight stanzas and 24 lines that opens with the sentence "A little less returned for him each spring." In response to the first line's invocation of both growth ("spring") and diminishment ("a little less"), I wrote and erased the poem repeatedly according to a set of simple instructions – a kind of script. The script went as follows: Write the poem on a piece of paper. Erase it. Write the poem on a second piece of paper, erase it, then rewrite it this time beginning one line down from the top and erase it again. Now, take a third piece of paper, do exactly what you did in the first two steps, then write and erase the poem a third time, this time beginning two lines down from the top of the page. And so on until 24 drawings have been made, every drawing in the series showing more erasures or a "little less" than the one before it.

Although I never sought to make *Poem Drawing* look like a landscape, the drawings as they evolved (especially the later ones) did begin to resemble one – the landscape of a Japanese dry garden, perhaps, full of clouds and mists and objects appearing and disappearing. In other words, the drawings resemble landscapes not in the conventional pictorial sense created by linear perspective, but rather in the sense of landscape as the densely layered space of an evolving palimpsest – landscape as we might understand it today. The drawings' evocation of place and atmosphere–their beauty, if one finds them beautiful–is, thus, not only a matter of appearance (the way the lines of the poem, for instance, may suggest multiple horizons), but is also borne of an open process: the process of repeatedly adding text (sedimentation) and subtracting it (erosion).

When will I finish *Poem Drawing*? Theoretically, I could have finished the drawings a long time ago. According to the drawing script, the project stops when the final drawing (# 24) contains the writing and erasure of the poem 24 times. But I take my time and only work on the project when I am moved to do so – and when I do work on the piece, I usually write and erase very slowly. Furthermore, since a part of me wants to keep the drawings "unfinished," it is quite likely that *Poem Drawing* will end when I cease to exist. However, because the drawing actions–writing and erasing the poem multiple times–are so simple and easy to emulate, they may well be re-enacted by someone else at some point in the future. This artist would write and erase Stevens's poem (or some other text), and then re-write and re-erase it again, and again, and again...In this way, the project may survive the limits of its first implementation and may continue to exist as an idea and open possibility.

1 From the early modern period I have in mind artists such as Braque, Picasso, Kurt Schwitters, as well as Marcel Duchamp. Later in the 20th century, numerous artists challenged the classical Western landscape tradition, including Robert Smithson, Anselm Kiefer, Maya Lin, Ann Hamilton, and David Hammons.

2 I met Peter and Anneliese Latz when they visited the University of Virginia, where I teach, in 2002.

1 A little less returned for him each spring.
2 Music began to fail him. Brahms, although
3 His dark familiar often walked apart.

4 His spirit grew uncertain of delight;
5 Certain of its uncertainty, in which
6 That dark companion left him unconsoled

7 For a self returning mostly memory.
8 Only last year he said that the naked moon
9 Was not the moon he used to see, to feel

10 (In the pale coherences of moon and mood
11 When he was young), naked and alien,
12 More leanly shining in a lonkier sky.

13 Its ruddy pallor had grown cadaverous.
14 He used his reason, exercised his will,
15 Turning in time to Brahms as alternate

16 In speech. He was that music and himself.
17 They were particles of order, a single majesty:
18 But he remembered the time when he stood alone.

19 He stood at last by God's help and the police;
20 But he remembered the time when he stood alone.
21 He yielded himself to that single majesty;

22 But he remembered the time when he stood alone,
23 When to be and delight to be used to be one,
24 Before the colors deepened and grew small.

Right: *Poem Drawing: A Little Less Returned for Him Each Spring, No. 1.*

IN CONVERSATION WITH
ELIZABETH K. MEYER

Elizabeth K. Meyer is Merril D. Peterson Professor of landscape architecture at the University of Virginia and founder of the UVA Center for Cultural Landscapes. Since the late 1980s, she has been a leading critic and theorist of landscape architecture, focused on materiality, experience, and contemporary cultural issues. In particular, Meyer has written and lectured extensively on beauty and aesthetics in landscape architecture, including her manifesto "Sustaining Beauty" (2008) and subsequent essay "Beyond Sustaining Beauty" (2015). In 2019, the *Journal of Landscape Architecture* dedicated an issue to Meyer's scholarship titled, "Sustaining Beauty and Beyond." Meyer is the recipient of numerous teaching awards, and was nominated by President Barack Obama to the US Commission of Fine Arts, where she served from 2012–2021. UVA alumnus **Colin Curley** caught up with Meyer on behalf of *LA+*.

+ You're well known for your scholarship on beauty and aesthetics in landscape architecture. What led you to explore those topics?

Two different things. The first is the class on theories of modern landscape that I was asked to create and teach at the [Harvard] GSD in the late 1980s. I was intrigued by a couple of recent articles written by Evelyn Bauer, Carolyn Constantine, and an earlier book by Peter Collins, where the picturesque was being described as the first cultural product of artistic modernity, and if you're talking about the picturesque, you have to start reading about aesthetics.

From that reading emerged the recognition that the picturesque was not just what something looked like, but one's experience of a place. You knew it was the beautiful, the picturesque, or the sublime because of how you *felt*, not just what you saw. That particular introduction to the sublime and awe was interesting because it raised the question whether it has anything to do with what we do now because we're not talking about the Alps, the Grand Canyon, a cathedral, or a mosque. It was really more me interrogating and excavating landscape history and trying to enrich our understanding of design theory that is still germane today. The link between the picturesque and the modern era was, of course, Robert Smithson's essay "The Monuments of the Passaic."

In the late 1990s when I had started teaching at UVA, I received an invitation from the faculty at the GSD to participate in an event related to Rich Haag that included an exhibition, a publication, and a trip to Seattle to meet Rich with a group of GSD students and Gary Hilderbrand. That experience with Rich changed the way I decided to write as a theorist and a critic. Part of it was that I had to communicate not just what I was learning about the Bloedel Reserve or Gasworks Park, but how I was feeling walking around and listening to Rich talk about them in real time. I was learning about the history of the site from him, but also recognizing this cognitive dissonance between what he was seeing and saying and what I was feeling. It made me realize, "Aha, I've got to write about this."

At the time, Kate Nesbitt, Jean-François Lyotard, and a group of other theorists, architects, and artists were writing about the post-modern and post-industrial sublime. I realized it mapped on to Rich's work beautifully because they were talking about an experience of awe, dread, uncertainty, vastness, and the infinite that wasn't about spatial vastness, but about temporal uncertainty.

To give an example of how that was affecting me, Rich spoke about "The time we pulled little Kitty's yellow slicker out of the lake, and it was eaten because of all the chemicals that were leaching into the water. We realized – 'we've got a plume,'" and about going around with a little pocketknife and scraping off the tar and crud that was oozing through the surface so that no one would see it. It was striking: this place just looks stable and yet it's alive. The surface and the subsurface are alive.

Opposite: Edge between two tree groves, Land Lab in Alnarp, Sweden.

It was a combination of me being super nerdy and reading primary source materials wondering, "What the heck did Smithson see in the picturesque that I wasn't taught?" going back to the sources where rack-and-ruin quarry landscapes were being described as picturesque in the 18th century, and then walking around with Rich, frankly that's how I got interested in aesthetics. Of course, whenever you haven't been taught something in school, you want to know what they were hiding from you, so part of it was that. You couldn't talk about feeling or aesthetics when I was in school, it was seen as girly and not serious.

+ I'd like to follow up on the post-industrial landscape sublime. It's a subject about which you've written extensively, and landscape architects increasingly work with post-industrial sites. Where and how do you draw the line between beauty and fetishization when it comes to disturbed, post-industrial sites?

I think the answer lies in getting beyond seeing the post-industrial as the ruins of architectural structures. There's a lot of fetishizing those and Nate Millington has written about it beautifully in terms of how Detroit's been documented by contemporary photographers.[1] I remember first bumping into this phenomenon while teaching in the late 1980s and early 1990s and being shocked that architectural ruins associated with the loss of jobs and the dislocation of neighborhoods were the ones that architects—particularly at the GSD—were obsessing about as objects.

The key for me lies in two things. The first I learned from Julie Bargmann when she joined our faculty at UVA in the mid-'90s, and appreciating how much her interest in those sites was connected to two things. One, that I think a lot of designers focus on, is an aesthetics of frugality where she wants to reuse everything on the site. I think that's a simple way to acknowledge that there's a material history on that site that in a previous generation would've been hauled off to the landfill somewhere else. It is actually the raw material for remaking the site.

The other part that Julie got increasingly interested in was seeing these sites as important spaces related to the history of labor. Who was working there, where were they living, what were they making, what stories were they telling? To think about the landscape as a memory device, both material memory and social personal memories, and then how that can be prompted, not narrated in its entirety. You can get a guidebook for that. What are the material remnants and the spatial configurations that are prompts to that memory?

That's where I think sites can be more enigmatic and less didactic, because the other side of fetishizing these objects is that they get interpreted through signs and exhibits that are so limiting. I guess I go back as a touchstone to Smithson. He says, "The landscape is a jumbled text. It's not coherent."[2] I think it's okay for there to be curiosities and juxtapositions, strange objects. Tim Morton talks about them as "strange strangers" that are simply prompts for knowing more or caring more.

The last thing about this—and the Norfolk Southern railroad accident in Ohio reminds us of this—is that there's real danger on a lot of post-industrial sites and that alone should be enough to give us pause about just celebrating the objects of their construction. We should understand the impact that contamination has had on communities, which I think gives one a little bit of empathy for other ways of interpreting these sites and for choreographing sequences so that you don't have access to everything, and danger is actually *felt* because of separation. When you're walking on a boardwalk over a dune at the beach you know it's to protect a dune. When you're walking on a boardwalk or scaffold on a post-industrial site, you know it's to protect you.

+ You've described beauty as being "connected to appearance but not exhausted by it." Could you elaborate a bit on your thoughts regarding form as it relates to beauty?

A lot of these questions surfaced for me between the time I wrote "Sustaining Beauty" and lectured on the piece, and when I wrote the follow-up discussing what I was hearing. One of the big disconnects I realized is that form, appearance, and aesthetics were understood by a lot of designers as synonyms, as meaning the exact same thing. Because of the shift toward performance and toward understanding the temporal aspect of our medium, which was very important, form started to get a bad word because you didn't want to be a formalist. You wanted the form to be coming out of something. As Anita Berrizbeitia has written so beautifully, all processes register in patterns on the ground and there's form there, so you can't ignore it.

Form has to do with configuration, material, and shaping; different from appearance, which is: "I'm looking at the form." Then in the history of aesthetics, there is a considerable amount of writing that describes aesthetics as a science of perception and related to feeling, and not the same as the thing that you're looking at. An aesthetic experience is connected to the thing which has an appearance, but to really understand the reason why it matters for design is to realize that the seeing and experience of the thing changes us.

There's a couple of ways to think about that. One, following Elaine Scarry and Alexander Nehamas, is to talk about the duration that an aesthetic experience takes. It doesn't mean it takes 10 minutes—it could even be a nanosecond—but what you see is filtered through what you know. The notion of universal beauty then gets called into question, because what you and I see is actually different. How we react to it is different based on our cultural backgrounds, where we've traveled, the experiences we've had.

Another way to think about it, which I find so exciting, is related to how since the 1980s (or the 1990s in art, in architecture, and design theory) there's been a recognition of the affectivity of experience, and how that is different from purely aesthetics. I got so excited by some of the reading on affectivity that Peter Connolly shared with me. Without getting into the weeds, the thing that was most powerful for me about those readings was recognizing that experiencing anything has the capacity to not only affect us phenomenologically but to change what we might do. That's where you get out of the "I feel this way, but maybe you don't feel the same," because affectivity has to do with an impulse or prompt to move.

The movement might be a change of what I value, but it may also be, "I value something so much that I have got to start doing something!" In a much sneakier, and also more probable way, if designers were more focused on the affectivity of what we're creating, we wouldn't have to worry about redesigning global systems. Don't get me wrong, I love all that big stuff, but if you have the capacity to prompt someone to change, to move, you're multiplying the things you care about in ways that we really need since climate change and everything else is going to require huge bottom-up changes in behavior.

This morning I had a meeting with a group of people who were advising me on the strategic plan we're doing for Morven Farm. One of the people is a cognitive psychologist who's done a lot of work on awe, and the way in which the experience of awe in nature actually has a huge impact on brain structure and how we relate to difference and confrontation and consensus – it just blows you away. These kinds of experiences—and they cannot be banal, they can't be generic beauty—have to be something that has the capacity to *hold* you for a minute so that you have that reaction. It's not about the pleasant. There are capacities for amplification of the impact of places that are way beyond ecosystem services.

What was so exciting is that after the meeting this psychologist sent me all of this recent empirically based research that I would never read on my own. All of a sudden I was looking at calculus formulas and it was so great to realize that the kinds of things that I might have intuited through reading in the humanities and philosophy are actually being substantiated through empirical research in the natural sciences.

This is a long way of saying that appearance matters a lot more than we think. It's not about just whether I like that form. It has the capacity to change not only who we are but how we might interact with others, and maybe even collectively find new ways of living together.

+ It's such a powerful and interesting way to think about the agency of landscape architecture. It may not be about co-opting expertise from other fields and thinking that we can do everything, but considering that what we can do, maybe, is to just move people through the way that we shape space.

This connects to Kate Soper's concept of alternative hedonism. In her essay, which is now a book, she discusses sustainability and sustainable practices.[3] For example, people who ride their bike to reduce their contributions to pollution. You could say that it's a hair shirt – you're just sacrificing. But what Soper says is that over time, your body feels differently, and you feel really good riding your bike, and you're getting an alternative pleasure out of that. You're interacting with the city or the countryside differently.

In her essay and book, she talks about changing environmental ethics, and how they lead to changing structures of feeling. That's a phrase that Raymond Williams used to describe that when ethics change, or paradigm shifts happen: it's not all in your head, there's actually a *structure of feeling*, like riding your bike to work. They're spatial practices we take on that are different because something has changed in our value system. Structures of feeling have spatial implications.

There's a little chain that I'm trying to construct here between, "I see something, I feel a certain way." What I feel is not just phenomenological, it is actually affecting me and changing what I might care about. It might be prompting me to move: maybe I'm a little lazy today, maybe it might take a few months. As many people in a community or generations start to feel that way, they start to change their daily routines. They have different spatial practices, and then all of a sudden landscape architects are thinking about how to begin to give form to those. The whole thing iterates.

+ When you wrote "Sustaining Beauty," it was a reaction to sustainable design discourse in landscape architecture. Now, discourse around the Anthropocene is inclined toward yet another form of that "extreme functionalism" about which you write on the one hand, and melancholia on the other. Do you see the Anthropocene as an aesthetic project for landscape architecture?

Yes. I haven't really started to give thought to it, but my students have. I speculated about it a little bit in a talk I gave at the ASLA headquarters about aesthetics and climate change, which isn't the same as the Anthropocene, but it was starting to deal with aesthetics and global implications.

That was the other reason why theories of affectivity interested me because of the word entanglement I was introduced to within that theoretical discourse. People in humanities are using a term that really came from quantum physics to talk about the way in which something afar can affect something near. If we're thinking about it in terms of quasi-objects, hyperobjects, or other ways of imagining the interconnections between our bodies and the world, I realized that entanglement was a way that allowed the toggling and the multi-scalar work that landscape architects do really well (better than a lot of other practitioners). It shifts focus from making a choice between big scale and body scale, by acknowledging that those are actually connected.

I can think of art projects that start to deal with this really well, like Andy Goldsworthy in the 1990s taking snow in rural England, making big snowballs, storing them in freezers, and then placing them in public spaces in London in June and July. As they melted, whatever was in the countryside – like lamb's wool and other detritus – floated through the city. Another is Olafur Eliasson, who has done these amazing light installations that are about experiencing things like a sunset inside museums. You can see that those are not just spectacles of light. People are seeing these installations in relationship to other things happening, and it's bringing one material reality to another place. But these are art projects. I think there are landscape versions of that, I just haven't done a lot of work thinking about it and I'm excited about what comes out of it.

+ The term entanglement certainly appears elsewhere in this journal issue. What do you mean when you use the term? Why does it matter for landscape architects?

From just a basic vocabulary word, I think about the difference between relationship, overlap, intersect. Those are terms that imply two things have a connection. But the word entanglement requires some forensics. It's complex, and it seems more apt for the multi-species spatial and material work we want to do; it seems more apt for the more-than-human obligation we have.

There was another article I just read today, I think it was in *The Atlantic*, about whale habitat. Turns out, they used to love being by the shore until we started mucking up the shore.[4] We're trying to protect habitat for them out in the ocean, but maybe they're a little more flexible. We took over their best place and so they had to find

another. The word entanglement for me is almost a metaphor for the humility we have to have, the depth of the research we need to do, and then the multi-scalar work that's necessary to even detail a small space, instead of thinking, "Oh, I did that in school, but we don't do that in practice." We also have to recognize that overlay maps don't cut it. They just don't. They have their value for other things, but they are not the solution to actually finding patterns and processes that are necessary for dealing with these entanglements.

I think there are words that show up to describe a concept in one field, and when they circulate to others, they take on different meanings and importance. "Entanglement" has a lot of promise for changing research methods and design processes. I've been thinking a lot about Anu Mathur in the last year. I think of the rigor, elegance, and just *pleasure* that one sees in the prints that she and Dilip da Cunha created over 20 years, and the correlation between the word entanglement and the work that it takes to actually decode that kind of representation. I think we live in a very sophisticated visual world, and we don't often give the public enough credit for understanding visual complexity. I don't think that those drawings, ideograms, and prints have to be relegated to just inside design conversations.

+ That's a good segue into the next question with regard to both representation and built work. Where do you see aesthetic innovation taking place in landscape architecture today?

One area where I'm in awe of what my students are doing—and maybe it's because I'm just such a technical luddite—is the graphic representation they've developed in the studios I've been teaching dealing with contested histories in public space. I've been assigning readings dealing with thick description that comes out of anthropology as well as Thaïsa Way's work, and I'm really taken with the way that students are finding techniques for including ghosts, memory, timelines, and change over time.

They're representations of places you know well like UVA's Academical Village, the Black Bus Stop, or places on the Downtown Mall near what was formerly Lee and Jackson Parks. They're relying on a lot of techniques that we introduce them to that Anu Mathur developed, but they're deploying them to a different end to try to hold contested memories and meanings.

I've found that they've actually been very good documents for opening up conversations with non-designers about these sites. They really resonated with a group of residents of a public housing project in a presentation we did before the pandemic. There was a walk from Friendship Court—the public housing project near the Downtown Mall—up to Lee Park, and there were a variety of ways in which that sequence was described from different points of view with the same kind of drawings. I think these more subjective modes of representing places are effective in finding the strange beauties that come out of them, or recognizing that someone's conception of beauty is a symbol of horror for someone else.

I'm also intrigued by the material explorations that are going on at the School of Architecture at UVA in terms of working with different forms of biomass. It's like this weird combination of Fred Flintstone meets CNC. We have a lot of students who are working in the [fabrication] lab here with several of the faculty on these material explorations. They're maybe not scalable yet; they're a little petite. How would they change the building industry? I don't know. But I'm really fascinated with the possibility of rethinking what we build with, and understanding the ways in which building processes may be more decentralized because of 3D printing and other technologies that are becoming more readily available.

There are a lot of other things I'd want to talk about, but I've only seen them in magazines – I need to get back to traveling.

+ Then we might be going back into the archives for the next question: if you had to nominate three projects for the honor of being the most beautiful works of landscape architecture, what would they be?

That was the one question I hoped I could just jettison. I'm not sure if I want to use the word *beauty*, but I do think there are places that have moved me because of their form and appearance. I did get to travel last week, and there was a plaza that was a public laundry in San Miguel de Allende that was so unbelievably moving because we're not familiar with domestic activities happening in public space. I'm going to guess this plaza was around 100 years old below an ancient spring and a high point at the town where there were public baths before and probably spiritual spring pilgrimages.

To see the repetition of 20 basins along the wall, beautifully sculpted, scaled for a couple of people, with the bottom shaped, deep at one end and shallow at the other. It was like someone had taken a motion Muybridge photo and concretized it in stucco. On two of the walls, there was placed a long bench, where you'd be waiting. There's just something amazing about a place where all of the program was given shape and form, and it was all within the structure of the walls. Then in the middle, a simple fountain that was not related at all. I was really struck by that.

On another note, because we've gotten our Barcelona program back up and running after the pandemic, it's been fun talking to students about the reactions they have had to Enric Miralles and Carme Pinós's work there – particularly the Olympic Archery Facility and the Igualada Cemetery. You can sense a similarity of fascination with the richness of a surface and an edge relative to the memory of, in that case, different kinds of bodies. Those two projects don't have fancy materials: one's stucco and one's concrete. The fact that the ground plane at the Igualada Cemetery includes materials that will decompose and that are not durable, that they're intended to decay – that's something that I saw for the first time 20 years ago, but it still really resonates; the Igualada Cemetery in particular, but also the archery grounds there.

Richard Haag's work is up there for me. He may have only created two totally awesome projects [the Bloedel Reserve and Gasworks Park] of a lot of others I don't know about, but hey, if I was so lucky to have created two places like that, I'd be pretty happy.

There are just so many others. I haven't seen anything that Field Operations has designed except for the High Line. I'm eager to see their work. I haven't seen a lot of MVVA's newer work at Tulsa. There are a lot of projects that look really interesting. Students who've seen the Core [City Park] Project in Detroit that Julie [Bargmann] worked on have also wowed.

I'll just leave you with one. This is the fourth and it's on my mind because of Morven. I should have started with this one. If I did a screen share and showed you my desktop background, it's of the Land Lab in Alnarp, Sweden. Alnarp is where the landscape architecture program is near Malmö–just north of Malmö and across the harbor from Copenhagen–and for 30 years, the landscape architecture students there have had the capacity on the edge of their agriculture campus to design and plant something. I don't know how big each of the plots are. They could be a quarter acre or half an acre, I'm not sure. Within them are every kind of version of a bosque, and a quincunx, and a grove, and a clump, and they're amazing – the spacing is different, the species are different. At a certain moment, a class started saying, "We want to change that one, not do another." There is a grove of *tilia* where a third of them were cut back to the ground. You have linden trees and then you have linden shrubs because they're suckering.

There's this combination of various experiences, the juxtaposition of each of them because they're a big long line, and then that changes over time. When I was there, Lisa Diedrich and others explained that the science students started doing fieldwork in the designed landscape versus in the fields and woodlots because they realized that the biodiversity was higher there than it was in the rest of the rural cultural landscape. That place is a combination of learning to design through actually understanding the medium: shaping the space, watching it over the years that you're in school, changing somebody else's design, having it measured and evaluated.

+ Is there anything we haven't discussed or something I missed that you would want a reader to take away from an interdisciplinary journal issue of landscape architecture on beauty?

Yes. I think it's great that landscape architects are thinking about challenging, questioning, and interrogating one aspect of our experiential relationship to form, and material to shape, which is beauty. But, between beauty and ugliness there's a whole array of other kinds of emotional and psychological responses that I think are really worth interrogating. Because it's not just beauty or I'm into performance, ecological performance – there's a whole array.

Students who've been doing work on queer theory in space have been interrogating categories of perception on the edge of ugliness, and what it means to be in spaces that are not about beauty or not beauty but something else. I think about Matthew Gandy's writings on queer theory and how it has a lot to offer urban ecology and urban landscape design. Another issue on the other aspects of aesthetic experience would be fantastic. Given the research on awe, awe might be worth interrogating as well – what is it that just makes us pause and wonder?

Opposite: Linden grove and linden coppice understory, Land Lab, Alnarp, Sweden.

1 Nate Millington, "Post-Industrial Imaginaries: Nature, Representation, and Ruin in Detroit, Michigan," *International Journal of Urban and Regional Research* 37, no. 1 (2013).

2 Robert Smithson, "A Sedimentation of the Mind: Earth Projects" (1968), https://holtsmithsonfoundation.org/sedimentation-mind-earth-projects.

3 Kate Soper, *Post-Growth Living: For an Alternative Hedonism* (Verso, 2020).

4 Emma Marris, "A Basic Premise of Animal Conservation Looks Shakier Than Ever," *The Atlantic* (23 February 2023), https://www.theatlantic.com/science/archive/2023/02/wild-animal-species-conservation-native-range-habitats/673153/.

NATURAL COSMETICS

Nicholas Holm

Nicholas Holm

Nicholas Holm

Nicholas Holm

Nicholas Holm

"I would like, he said with his deadpan comic style, the fields tinged with red, the rivers yellow, and the trees painted blue. Nature has no imagination."[1]

NICHOLAS HOLM

Nicholas Holm is a cultural theorist and a senior lecturer in media studies at Massey University in Aotearoa, New Zealand. He holds a PhD in English from McMaster University. Holm's research explores the political and social consequences of popular aesthetics across a range of cultural contexts including humor, advertising, and our relation to non-human animals and systems.

+ CULTURAL THEORY

Viewed from space, the colors of an algal bloom trace complex, delicate lines across the flow of an ocean current: like the whorls and clouds that follow a painter's brush dipped in water reimagined on a maximalist scale. As might be expected, there are many possible shades of green–artichoke, fern, forest, mantis, and myrtle–but also elsewhere thick, rich, shades of carmine red, and even stunning blue bioluminescence when and where the conditions are right. Seeping across seas and lakes, algal blooms provide the substrate for patterns that can extend across miles of open water or transform foreshores into flamboyant and other-worldly tableau. By virtue of their vibrant colors and flowing organic shapes, there is certainly a theoretical argument to be made that these environmental phenomena are viable candidates for aesthetic contemplation: examples of the power of nature to inspire and delight. And yet, in practice, few would appear to take the time to reflect on the beauty of an algal boom (or at least not dare do so in too public a forum).

An algal bloom is caused by a "sudden, rapid and perceptible increase in phytoplankton biomass."[2] Such phenomena can and do occur independent of human intervention but are increasingly and frequently linked with anthropogenic causes: in particular, industrial effluent, urban wastewater, and nutrient runoffs from agriculture. Although not always toxic, most news and governmental reports tend to (understandably) focus upon those blooms that pose a threat to marine and human life or can be linked with the warming ocean caused by climate change.[3] As a result, algal blooms tend to be understood not as forms of potential beauty, but as evidence of the harmful, even deadly, consequences of human interference – deeply ugly symptoms of a natural world increasingly and worryingly out of kilter. They are not perceived as works of art, but rather as crimes against nature.

The thwarted beauty of the algal bloom is indicative of the oddly specific aesthetic regime that structures our judgements of natural and nature-adjacent beauty. The aesthetic appraisal of nature (what scholars in the area tend to refer to as the nonhuman or more-than-human world) is never simply just a matter of accounting for sensual, formal, affective qualities. Even though some might argue that judgments of aesthetics ought to be separated from considerations of ethics,[4] in practice, such appraisals are almost invariably tied up with deeper assumptions regarding what belongs and what does not. As the case of the algal bloom demonstrates, in order to be deemed beautiful it is insufficient for a natural entity to just appeal to the senses. Instead, it must also–for want of a better word–fit: it must exist in ways, places, and relationships that are thought to be appropriate. The beauty of nature is not only about what strikes the senses, but also what is perceived as the correct and proper, sometimes figured as "healthy," arrangement of nature's constituent elements and processes.

It is in order to make sense of this situation that I'd like to propose the concept of "natural cosmetics." In relation to questions of beauty, cosmetics carries about it the whiff of superficiality and frivolous ornamentation. No doubt this is in large part a result of gendered practices and expectations around cosmetics as both a type of consumer good and surgical practice.[5] The historical expectation that women ought to alter their appearance to better meet social expectations–while also being simultaneously pilloried as vain or deceptive for doing exactly that–has meant that cosmetics has come to be perceived as a sort of lesser or false form of beauty. To describe something or someone as beautiful in a cosmetic sense is to invoke a distinction between appearance and essence. It is to suggest that the beauty being considered is only "skin-deep" in comparison to an imagined standard of authentic, or so-called "natural," beauty. This is not, however, the idea of beauty that I want to argue is appropriate to an algal bloom: the last thing I'm seeking to suggest is that this is a deceptively pleasing appearance plastered atop what is better understood as a form of corruption. Rather, the cosmetics of the algal bloom are important insofar as they can help us understand a more complex, and I think also more profound, account of how aesthetic judgements of nature are conceived and executed.

The current connotations of cosmetics far from exhaust the term's possible or historical meanings. Our contemporary usage of the word cosmetics–to describe the application of chemical compounds to change the appearance of one's face or body–is derived from the Greek word *kosmētikos*. This is usually translated as "skilled in ordering or arranging." Thus, in an etymological sense, cosmetics is not so much the beauty of adornment, as of the proper arranging of one's comportment. Furthermore, this meaning is, in turn, a derivation of *kósmos*, which refers to a system that is not just arranged, but arranged in a way that is proper, orderly, and lawful. It is from this meaning that we gain our concept of the cosmos: an account of the universe, following the ancient Greek scientist Pythagoras, as a complex but ordered system where everything fits together and has its own place.[6] The concept of cosmetic beauty, as I'm proposing it, thus also carries within it a secondary, neglected

meaning that points toward how beauty can become entangled with a sense of order and propriety. In the context of natural beauty, therefore, cosmetic beauty is not only something that pleases the senses, but that does so while also occupying a proper position in a functioning natural system.

Although potentially jarring for a contemporary reader, the suggestion that beauty may be dependent on systematic order–not the order of internal composition, but rather the order of a universe where everything is where it is meant to be–is neither a recent nor incidental development in aesthetic thought. Indeed, an appeal to order sits at the foundation of Western aesthetic thought as manifested in the writing of Immanuel Kant. Insofar as it makes sense to identify any one book as the cornerstone of how we think and talk about beauty, that book is Kant's *Critique of the Power of Judgment*,[7] which lays out a framework of taste and transcendence, autonomy, and subjectivity that persists in the deep wiring of ongoing scholarly and everyday conversations about topics like art and aesthetics. And for Kant, nature comes before art as the foundational human experience of beauty–"art can only be called beautiful if we are aware that it is art and yet it looks to us like nature"[8]–exactly to the extent that nature presents what he refers to as a "lawful arrangement"[9] that exists beyond the human and which, he argues, inspires a moral orientation toward the world.[10] Kant refers to this experience in terms of the "purposiveness" of nature,[11] but we need not spend too long with this term (which also carries the risk of evoking the ire of more serious Kant scholars), to appreciate how this idea can help illuminate the cosmetic failure of the algal bloom and indeed other forms of nature that are thought to be out of place.

Although the terms by which Kant expresses this aspiration for aesthetic order might seem somewhat alien to current attitudes, the underlying perspective it expresses is not: to be regarded as beautiful, the natural world needs to be correctly arranged. Natural elements, from plants and animals to landscape features, are typically only aesthetically appreciated when they are located where they are "meant" to be.[12] Encountered elsewhere, they can be unsettling, threatening, or corrupting.[13] Importantly, while often aligned with scientific ecology, this cosmetic order cannot be reduced to it: the sparrow is in no way "native" to London, but has nonetheless been embraced as a true citizen of the British capital since the time of Dickens. When their numbers began to decline in the early 2000s, this was experienced as a loss: the disappearance of a species that, in some deep way, was felt as if it were meant to be there. It is against this backdrop of cosmetic assumptions that a beautiful plant out of place becomes a weed.[14] A majestic animal out of place becomes a disruption. On a larger scale, to transform an environment too far from its "correct" state (what might tautologically be referred to as its natural state)—by removing vegetation, redirecting rivers, draining swamps—is to run the risk of ruining it, of reducing it to "wasteland": a term that captures the twinned ethical and aesthetic failures of nature that exists outside of the correct order.[15] When we assess the aesthetic merits of nature, it is with respect to an inherited, over-arching, and often unexamined, sense of cosmetic order. One in which the algal bloom finds little space to belong.

There is, however, a wrinkle to this formulation: it is difficult to identify a single immutable and correct order by which nature ought to be arranged. Ideas of beauty are subject to change,[16] as are accounts of the natural order.[17] This much becomes apparent if we return our consideration to Immanuel Kant, who studiously maintained his daily walk through the fields surrounding the small Prussian city Konigsberg, but also famously never travelled any farther beyond the place of his birth.[18] What would such a man—who never experienced an environment not shaped by decades, if not centuries, of sustained, directed human toil[19]—know about the arrangements of any thoroughly natural world? There is no threat of wilderness intruding here. Rather, for Kant, the distinction between the natural and the artificial was philosophized in terms of that between an organic and an artificial flower;[20] between instrumentally simulated birdsong versus that of a biological bird.[21] When Kant speaks of the lawful arrangement of nature, we can therefore imagine he speaks of tilled fields and managed forests, rather than the pure untrammeled expanses of the Amazon rainforest or Southern Ocean that now populate our environmental dreams. For that worldview, nature in its correct place is a well-maintained paddock, rather than untouched wilderness.

Kant's vision of a properly ordered nature was very much of his era. The 18th century was an age of "improvement," when beliefs regarding the correct state of the natural world were caught up with assumptions of Christian morality and capitalist productivism.[22] According to this logic of improvement, the unproductive could not be beautiful. In contrast to our forebears, in contemporary Western society we now have a much more fine-grained account of our preferred cosmetic order (which is not to say, though, that we necessarily possess a better or more ontologically accurate account). Informed by ecological and environmental sciences, our contemporary cosmetic vision for the natural world is more empirically sophisticated and more attuned to the wider, hidden networks of cause-and-effect that underpin non-human systems. It is also admirably less anthropocentric (or perhaps, more accurately, less theocentric): it seeks to create space to appreciate the value of the natural world in ways that do not reduce it to raw material for human use

and exploitation. However, it nonetheless remains a relatively rigid system that assumes that under ideal conditions–when everything is as it should be–certain species ought to inhabit certain environments in certain numbers arranged according to certain relationships. The transition from an economic-ethical orientated cosmetics to one informed by notions of ecology and environmentalism has transformed our shared sense of the proper order of nature, but a sense of the proper nonetheless persists. And importantly, this is not simply a scientific and rational but also a deeply aesthetic set of beliefs.

The concept of cosmetics helps us understand the extent to which claims about the environment are never entirely scientific – they always carry a touch of the aesthetic. Several important points follow from this. Not least that conservationists are as much cosmetic technicians as they are ecological managers. When they help revive populations of endangered species, restore the flow of rivers, or remove toxic waste from an environment, conservation practitioners are not just returning ecosystems to more "pristine" conditions, but in doing so, are making an aesthetic intervention that renders them beautiful according to conventional cosmetic standards. This observation is not meant to trivialize their work–beauty is incredibly important–but rather to shed light on a too-often overlooked aspect of such practices, which are overwhelmingly characterized as scientific, rather than aesthetic, interventions. However, they are not only (or even) "repairing" damage. They are making use of technological tools to restore the natural world to its previous appearance: pest-trapping and replanting as ecological Botox to help an environment get back its looks from when it was young(er) and pretty.

Acknowledging the aesthetic-cosmetic elements of ecological practice also acts to undermine long-standing distinctions between ecological and landscape practice. It does this not by asserting that design ought to be subordinated to "natural" processes,[23] but rather by suggesting that ecological actions may be more aesthetic than their champions would usually like to consider. Framed in this way, beauty is not simply an element that ought to be considered in discussions of landscape, but rather one that we cannot help but consider, because it is baked into our ecological thinking in ways that we are not accustomed to notice or realize. Thus, the question is not whether or not beauty is "sustained" but whether or not it is done so consciously and explicitly. Approached in this way, the choice is less between nature and culture understood as distinct and opposed principles,[24] and more about whether an environmental intervention aligns or breaks with the prevailing cosmetic order. Does it put things back "where they belong," or instead choose to scatter the pieces and color outside the lines?

1 Jules Levallois, *Memoire d'un Critique* (Librairie Illustrée, 1895), 93 (author's translation). Although this quotation is usually directly attributed to Charles Baudelaire, the only formal recording is Levallois's memory of Baudelaire's remark.

2 S. L. Sarkar, *Marine Algal Bloom* (Springer, 2018), 1–2.

3 Jeremy Hance, "Lethal algae blooms – an ecosystem out of balance," *The Guardian* (January 4, 2020); Clare Davis, "Bloom or Bust," *Nature Reviews Earth & Environment* 2, no. 447 (2021); David Mack, "How To Protect Yourself (And Your Dogs) From Toxic Blue-Green Algae This Summer," *Buzzfeed News* (May 19, 2022); Amber Allott, "Fears climate change could tip toxic algae to deadly levels," *Stuff.co.nz* (January, 17 2022); Priya Shula, "'Red Tides' Are Currently Blooming In Southern California," *Forbes* (April 30, 2022).

4 Mark Trieb, "Ethics ≠ Aesthetics," *Journal of Landscape Architecture* 13, no.2 (2018): 30–41.

5 Autumn Whitefield-Madrano, *Face Value: The Hidden Ways Beauty Shapes Women's Lives* (Simon & Schuster, 2016); Naomi Wolf, *The Beauty Myth* (Chatto & Windus, 1990).

6 Philip Sidney Horky, "When did *Kosmos* become the *Kosmos*?" in Philip Sidney Horky (ed.), *Cosmos in the Ancient World* (Cambridge University Press, 2019), 22–41.

7 Immanuel Kant, *Critique of the Power of Judgement*, trans. by Paul Huyer & Eric Matthews (Cambridge University Press, 2000).

8 Ibid., 185.

9 Ibid., 181.

10 Ibid., 242–78; 293–301.

11 Hannah Ginsborg, "Kant's Aesthetics and Teleology," *Stanford Encyclopedia of Philosophy*, https://plato.stanford.edu/entries/kant-aesthetics/#3.1.

12 There is, of course, some scope for variation in how these factors are experienced: it is a tendency, rather than a rule.

13 David Gissen, *Subnature: Architecture's Other Environments* (Princeton Architectural Press, 2009), 210.

14 Ibid., 150.

15 Vittoria Di Palma, *Wasteland: A History* (Yale University Press, 2014), 9.

16 Elizabeth K. Meyer, "Beyond 'Sustaining Beauty'," in M. Elen Denning (ed.), *Values in Landscape Architecture and Environmental Design* (Louisiana State University Press, 2018), 30–53, 33.

17 Elizabeth K. Meyer, "Sustaining Beauty. The Performance of Appearance," *Journal of Landscape Architecture* 3, no. 1 (2012): 6–23, 20.

18 Frédéric Gros, *A Philosophy of Walking*, trans. by John Howe (Verso, 2014), 153–56.

19 Andrei Levchenkov, "Changes in the Cultural Landscape of the Kaliningrad Region's Periphery in the 19th/20th Centuries," *Baltic Region* 1, no. 8 (2016): 93, 96–98.

20 Kant, *Critique of the Power of Judgement*, 179.

21 Ibid., 182.

22 Di Palma, *Wasteland*, 43–44.

23 Ian McHarg, *Design with Nature* (John Wiley & Sons, 1969).

24 Imke van Hellemondt & Bruno Notteboom, "Sustaining beauty and beyond," *Journal of Landscape Architecture*, 13, no. 2 (2018): 4–7.

25 Antoine Picon (trans. Karen Bates), "Anxious Landscapes: From the Ruin to Rust," *Grey Room* 1 (2000): 64–83.

Such a question is increasingly urgent in a world being reshaped by climate change and other anthropogenic forces, where it is increasingly difficult to disentangle the influences of human and nonhuman factors. Even in the absence of the human touch, the natural world is fundamentally dynamic, and humanity's influence only exacerbates this quality. Such rapid change threatens to play havoc with the cosmetic order of things: as hunting ranges expand and contract, oceans rise and warm, and populations of animals are displaced. Unfortunately, as a set of principles cosmetic aesthetics provide little of the guidance that we need when accounting for the possibility of change in (no longer quite so) natural environments. When something appears where it is not expected, it is not encountered as a miracle but rather as an affront. Deviations from expectations are thus understood as something to be corrected: sometimes with lethal force. The cosmetic order means that we are unable to appreciate the aesthetic appeal of the potentially beautiful animal, plant, or landscape feature that appears out of place. In such a situation, a cosmetic aesthetics of nature therefore becomes insufficient and even potentially regressive when it cannot account for the possibility of multiple arrangements that emerge in the context of a shifting world.

What would it mean, then, to imagine the possibility of natural aesthetics beyond our inherited cosmetic order? And what might this mean for the beauty of the algal bloom? Doing so would require an account of natural beauty not so beholden to assumptions of stable order: one that would open up the possibility of finding natural beauty in new forms and space, including urban and other unnatural environments that depart from an inherited vision of the ideal order of nature.[25] This cannot mean "anything goes," however – the canvas of the natural world is too essential for our continued survival as a species to permit the widescale use of pollutive reagents. Art cannot be just for art's sake on a planetary level if we want to continue to have water to drink and air to breathe. But, also, we have to move beyond cosmetics if we are to ever find value (and dignity and beauty) in the landscapes that we, as humans, have already altered. In that spirit, what would it mean to think of the algal bloom as more than just a disaster, but instead to appreciate it as a collaborative work of art between human and nonhuman forces, painting across the water with blooms that are not just a toxin, but themselves living parts of their own ecosystem? Rethinking natural beauty beyond cosmetics encourages not only a reassessment of the formal pleasures of the algal bloom, but also a more profound re-examination of the deeper entanglement of aesthetic and ecological thought and the ways that shapes larger ideas regarding what constitutes desirable forms of environment, nature, and landscape.

IMAGE CREDITS

In Conversation with Elizabeth K. Meyer

p. 94: "Edge between two tree groves" (2016) by Elizabeth Meyer, used with permission.

p. 99: Thick section, topographies of belonging and exclusion, student work by Rebecca Hinch, Jingling Lai, and Xioaxuan Ren (2020). Instructors Sara Jacobs, Michael Ezban, Elizabeth Meyer.

p. 103: "Linden grove and linden coppice understory" (2016) by Elizabeth Meyer, used with permission.

Natural Cosmetics

p. 104–111: Images by Zicheng Kai Zhao, used with permission.

LA+

A vast network of material and informational exchanges link botany to landscape design. As we scan nursery catalogs to select our favorite species and cultivars for a proposed design, much is concealed or forgotten about the seedy histories of colonization of which plant breeding, trade, and botanic gardens have played a central role. The blossoming interest in plants among environmental historians, science studies scholars, philosophers, and others are shedding light on these entanglements. **LA+ BOTANIC** considers our evolving relationship with plants with contributors reflecting on what new natures and people-plant relations are being materialized in plant breeding, plant conservation, botanic garden design, and botanic art today. Guest-edited by Karen M'Closkey, contributors include:

GIOVANNI ALOI

IRUS BRAVERMAN

PATRICK BLANC

XAN SARAH CHACKO

SONJA DÜMPELMANN

JARED FARMER

ANNETTE FIERRO

MATTHEW GANDY

URSULA K. HEISE

ANDREA LING

JANET MARINELLI

KAREN M'CLOSKEY

BERONDA L. MONTGOMERY

CATHERINE MOSBACH

KATJA GRÖTZNER NEVES

BONNIE-KATE WALKER

OUT SPRING 2024

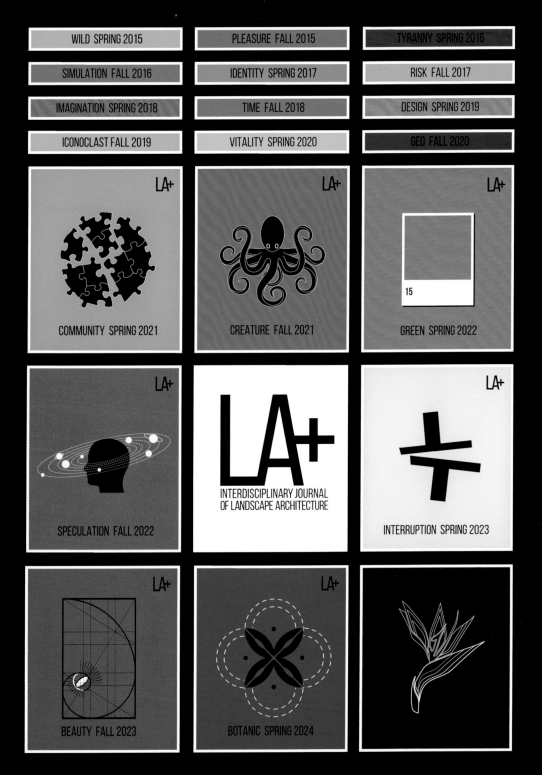

LA+ (Landscape Architecture Plus) from the University of Pennsylvania Weitzman School of Design is the first truly interdisciplinary journal of landscape architecture. Within its pages you will hear not only from designers, but also from historians, artists, philosophers, psychologists, geographers, sociologists, planners, scientists, and others. Our aim is to reveal connections and build collaborations between landscape architecture and other disciplines by exploring each issue's theme from multiple perspectives.

LA+ brings you a rich collection of contemporary thinkers and designers in two issues each year. To subscribe follow the links at WWW.LAPLUSJOURNAL.COM.